The ROAD TO Freedom

A Young Refugee's Journeys

ALBERT TANG

THE ROAD TO FREEDOM
A YOUNG REFUGEE'S JOURNEYS

iUniverse books may be ordered through booksellers or by contacting:

iUniverse
1663 Liberty Drive
Bloomington, IN 47403
www.iuniverse.com
844-349-9409

ISBN: 978-1-6632-1161-3 (sc)
ISBN: 978-1-6632-1160-6 (e)

Library of Congress Control Number: 2021901380

Print information available on the last page.

iUniverse rev. date: 02/23/2021

To my maternal grandparents, Ah Gong
and Ah Ma, who raised me and taught me
to be fair and stand against injustice

To my parents, who sacrificed so much
for me, taught me the value of hard
work, and allowed me to be myself

CONTENTS

ACKNOWLEDGMENTS

I want to give a special thanks to Mr. Ly, our family sponsor; Ms. Margaret McComb; and Barbara and John Moor, who helped make our New Zealand transition easier and became dear friends to us.

Acknowledgments also go to Mr. Boscawen, Ms. Cleary, and Mr. Singh of Otahuhu College, Auckland, New Zealand, for their encouragement and guidance; the UNHCR and International Red Cross for helping refugees like me; and, last but not least, my dear wife, who trusts me and loves me. She made me a better person than I could ever be on my own.

INTRODUCTION

One morning in 1970 when I was about five years old, I could recall vividly it was not a regular day. When I opened our front door, I saw a group of armed soldiers had arrived to guard the perimeter of the school where we lived. This not only signaled the beginning of the Cambodian civil war, but it also led to the Cambodian atrocities and genocide by dictator Pol Pot's communist regime.

The fact that I am still alive and able to write this book makes me feel like I am the luckiest person. I know not many people in a lifetime could have the opportunity to have personally lived and experienced what life was like under the world's most brutal communist dictator, Pol Pot (Khmer Rouge), where a country's currency system was abolished overnight.

Not only were all its city dwellers, like my family and me, forced to do hard labor in the countryside, but we were also starved and treated as dispensable people. During the four-year reign, about two million people died by starvation or were killed by the Khmer Rouge. My family and I miraculously survived the four-year ordeal. We trekked through minefields and became refugees in Thailand. And within a few short years, my life was completely changed. I was not only so blessed with a chance to get a world-class education, but I also was given an opportunity to live and work in the world's most admired and blessed region, the San Francisco Bay Area.

I know to many people I am just a regular Joe, your coworker, or your neighbor. But to me, what I currently have, my family and my freedom, is much more precious, and I could not take it for granted. All this was possible to me because I have been so fortunate to meet many kind and caring people along my journey. And I forever owe my gratitude to all of them.

I had been sharing anecdotes of my story to quite a few people. Many of my narratives began when someone asks me, "Where are you from?" Sometimes I would recount an event I either personally experienced or witnessed during a group luncheon with coworkers. I noticed very often I quickly became the focal point of the table. And soon we would overrun our lunch break by an hour or two. But more importantly, everyone had a good time.

Over the years, quite a few friends who were willing to listen to my stories encouraged me to document them. For the longest time, I did not take it seriously because I thought they were just being courteous. Anyway, like most people, I need my day job to pay the bills, and it keeps me occupied twelve to fourteen hours per day. I rarely have any time or energy to pursue other interests. So writing a book was never in my mind or a priority.

My work calls for me to fly across the Pacific frequently, at least once a quarter or sometimes once a month. A one-way flight from San Francisco to North Asia cities normally takes eleven to fourteen hours, depending on my destination. I have many hours to burn during the flight. When I was younger, on most flights I would enjoy my in-flight meal, watch a movie, and doze off before I could finish the movie. By the time I woke up, the flight would be preparing for landing.

But in the past couple of years, the same eleven to fourteen hours seemed to last much longer. It was becoming harder and harder for me to sleep on a plane unless I was fortunate enough to get a free upgrade to business class. I guess it is just part of the natural aging process. Nonetheless, I needed to find something to kill time and make the long flight more bearable. With the extra free time to burn, I started to type bits and pieces of my story on my PDA, and before long I had eighty-plus pages.

And without further ado, welcome aboard. Please put on your seatbelt, buckle up, and enjoy the ride.

One

The Coup and Civil War

My mom and dad were both teaching at a boarding school in Kampong Cham, a provincial city located just northeast of the capital, Phnom Penh, Cambodia. Many students were from rural villages where there was no school and it was too far for them to commute to school daily. Many teachers in this school were also from out of town. So the school was also providing living quarters for teachers. Since Mom and Dad were both out-of-town teachers, we got a bigger living unit for four persons (Mom, Dad, my younger brother, and me).

We were considered a middle-class family by local standards. We had a good and peaceful life, I would say. During the week while Mom and Dad were teaching at school, they hired a nanny to come and take care of us within the school. I was accustomed to the school life.

Each day, the school started at 9:00 a.m. And by 10:00 a.m., I would hear the school bell ring and see the kids rush out of the classroom and play happily in the schoolyard. The school bell would ring again about ten minutes later, signaling the morning break had ended. The kids and teachers alike would return to the classroom.

After school, our nanny would return my brother and me to my parents. On weekends, my parents would take us to swim in the river or see movies. During the longer summer holiday, my parents would bring us to visit my grandparents in Kampot, about two hundred kilometers away.

In 1970 when I was about five years old, a military coup broke out in the capital city, Phnom Penh. A military strong man named Lon-Noh initiated a coup to overthrow the crown prince, Norodom Sihanouk, while Sihanouk was out of the country. Prince Sihanouk had been Cambodia's head of state since gaining independence from France in 1953. But his foreign policies were increasingly leaning toward China, under communist strongman Mao Ze Dong, which caused concern in Washington. There had been suspicion and accusations that the US government played some role in the overthrow of Sihanouk in their effort to slow down communist advance in Indochina (Vietnam, Cambodia, and Lao).

This coup in Phnom Penh completely changed my life. I was too young to know what was happening outside, but I could remember vividly that it was not a regular day because it was past 8:00 a.m. and the school ground was unusually quiet. On a normal weekday, it would be bustling with kids and teachers alike rushing to their respective classes.

Today, both my parents were still at home, and Mom was feeding us breakfast in the house. After breakfast, Dad went out while Mom, my brother, and I stayed home. Mom would not allow us to go out of the house to play. By noon, Dad returned and told us it was OK to go outside to play. But we were to just stay within the school grounds and never go out to the street.

My brother and I happily ran outside and played. Once we were out in the schoolyard, I saw many soldiers guarding the school perimeter, standing about fifty meters apart, and each carried a gun over their shoulder. As a young boy, I had been playing with toy guns. I was curious.

I wanted to go and see the real gun, so I asked Mom, "Can I please get closer to the fence to see the soldiers?"

Mom quickly pulled me in. "No! It is not safe." It was as if she knew what was happening outside.

Soon it was lunchtime, and we did not go to the teacher cafeteria for lunch like we normally did. Mom fed us with whatever she could find in the house. As my brother and I were eating our lunch, we saw Dad coming back.

He updated us. "It is crazy out there. We cannot go out of the school."

Mom asked, "Were you able to go out and see what was happening?"

Dad replied, "Not really. I can only get as far as the school's main gate. The soldiers told me nobody was allowed to leave the school."

The school was a Chinese school. There was suspicion by the Lon-Noh new government that pro-China or procommunist elements were among the teachers and students in this Chinese school. About a hundred Lon-Noh's soldiers were sent to guard the perimeter of the school to make sure no school residents were able to leave. They might be waiting for order to come down to go into the school, to search and arrest the procommunist element. In 1970, many Cambodians were very loyal to Prince Sihanouk, especially the rural Cambodians. And the farmers in Kampong Cham province were the strongest opposition against the coup.

Back to the school, by early afternoon, we started to hear a big group of protesters chanting and marching in our direction. This was the start of an uprising or beginning of a Cambodian civil war. The chanting was getting louder and louder as the protesting farmers moved closer to the school. From our window, we could see the soldiers started to retreat as they saw too many protesters were approaching, and the soldiers figured if the protesters turned on them, they could not stop the assault.

One by one, the soldiers abandoned their posts and ran away from the school perimeter. Soon the protesters were marching and chanting right outside the school gate. It was a big crowd, at least several hundred people, and all looked very angry. Many protesters were chanting and waving homemade signs, posters, and banners of various sizes. A few men on the front line held up a big banner as they marched forward.

I was too young to read what the sign said. All I could tell were some signs had a cartoon of someone's head being chopped by an ax. A few carried a big poster of our beloved Prince Sihanouk, and other people simply carried the Cambodian national flag. Many protesters also carried different kinds of farm tools (hoes, spades, machetes, axes, etc.). We thought the protesters were going to enter the school.

Instead, after a short pause, they continued their march along the main street, heading to the Kampong Cham city center.

After the protesters marched away toward the city center, the school residents came out to check on one another. Some went to check on their friend units; others checked on their neighbors.

"How are you guys? Are you guys OK? What about the Channi family?"

It was now late in the afternoon. The school ground and nearby street were peaceful again. Dad went out to check. He returned approximately ten minutes later and said, "Everything is back to normal now. Let's go and eat out tonight."

My brother and I were so excited and could not wait to go out for dinner. My parents took us out to a nearby restaurant about two blocks away from the school. As we were walking to the restaurant, Mom held our hands, my brother on her left and me on her right. We were so excited and tried to check out every little thing along the way. Sometimes I pulled right; other times my brother would pull left. Each time Mom pulled us straight back.

Normally there were many shops and restaurants on both sides of the street. But today I noticed some stores were closed. Only a few businesses were open. Anyway, soon we got to our favorite restaurant, and we had an enjoyable meal and returned home after dinner.

The protest by farmers in Kampong Cham continued on day two without any local government intervention. Many businesses and the school could not open until this unrest was resolved. The next morning, day three, things seemed to go back to normal. We went to the teacher's cafeteria to have breakfast.

After breakfast, I noticed our nanny had not shown up to take care of us. My parents also did not go to teach. Instead both were reading some books at home. By midmorning, I started to hear the chants of protesters again coming from a distance, and the chanting would get louder and louder as they were approaching the school again. The protesters were chanting as they walked past the school and marched toward the city center.

Dad commented, "I don't know how long this protest will go on. Until then, we cannot open the school."

For the next two to three hours, things were quiet at the school. My brother and I were allowed to play in the schoolyard while Mom could still see us from the window, and we were happy.

Then the silence was broken up by the sound of many rounds of machine-gun shootings, *pop pop pop pop*, from a distance. Mom hurriedly jumped out, pulled us back into the house, and locked the door. We learned later Lon-Noh's new government in Phnom Penh had sent out reinforcement, tanks and armed soldiers, to suppress the protest in Kampong Cham.

The sound of machine-gun firing, *pop pop pop pop*, went on and off and on again for about twenty more minutes. We could hear the crying, the screaming for help, by the protesters. It echoed for blocks. This went on for the whole afternoon as we hid inside the house.

As night fell, Dad went out to see other teachers at the school. I guess they were discussing what to do next: to continue to stay at school or to leave the school and go back to each person's hometown. Mom put us to bed early that night.

The next morning, Mom prepared breakfast for us while Dad went out to check. Dad returned about ten minutes later and said, "I heard they had killed hundreds of protesters yesterday. The situation on the street was very tense. We must leave now while we still have a chance."

I had no idea where we were going. All I remembered was that we went to take the bus and we later arrived at my grandparents' house some two hundred kilometers away in Kampot. To me, wow, this was much better than I had expected. I always loved to visit my grandparents. Grandma was a very good cook, and there were always plenty of goodies to eat.

Every summer during the school holiday, my parents always brought us to visit our grandparents. We normally stayed there for a week or two. There was always plenty of fun stuff to do at my grandparents' place. We would go fishing along the river or the seashore. Other times, my uncle, my brother, and I would ride a bike. Sometimes we simply ran and played in the backyard with other kids.

A few days later, I saw my dad was about to leave my grandparents' place. He said goodbye to us, just like he always had. Nothing was unusual about this. Sometimes he had to go back to the school first. I figured we would see him again in the next few days, back home at the school.

One morning about a week later, Mom and her younger sister were about to go out. I asked Mom if my brother and I could come along. But Mom said, "No, you go and play with your brother."

I tried to negotiate with her, like "How about just me?" I was thinking maybe if it were just me, it would not be as much a burden for her.

But Mom replied gently, "No, you need to stay and take care of your brother."

I never realized that she actually was serious when she said that. That was the last time my brother and I saw and heard from our mom and dad for the next nine years. We had no idea why our parents left us behind, where they went, or what happened to them. I could only assume that no parent would do anything to hurt their young children, and my parents made that decision very painfully at the time. And maybe the Lon-Noh government was planning to arrest any procommunist element in the school. Fortunately for us, the protesters came by early, and we had a chance to escape. This would explain the reason why my parents hurriedly took us to my grandma's place, I guess to hide.

I could only guess that my parents thought they could be arrested anytime. And if they got arrested, they did not want my brother and me to be dragged down as well. This was why they left us with Grandma. If my parents were arrested, best case, they would be sent to prison. Worst case, they might get killed. After all, this was wartime in Cambodia.

I guess my parents must have strongly believed in their heart that it was in our best interest to stay with my grandparents for the time being. As you read on, you will see that given the situation at the time, nobody could foresee what was going to happen or offer any assurance that my family would be better off if my parents were to make a different decision.

During the civil war, Cambodia was divided into two regions: cities and rural areas. Many cities were under Lon-Noh's government control; the majority of rural areas, between cities, were controlled by the Khmer Rouge, or Cambodian communist party, who were fighting against the government.

After our mom's departure, like any young kid at that age—five for me and four for my brother—we were traumatized by this experience. We would cry every day asking for Mom and Dad. Sometimes one of us cried first, and the other followed. Other times we simply cried together.

Each time we were comforted or lied to. "They will come back soon (or tomorrow or next week)." And each time they never returned. Each night my younger brother would ask me for Mom or Dad, and I did not know what to do. Initially all I could do was cuddle and sob with him quietly together until we fell asleep.

Some nights he asked, "Why did Mom abandon us? Was I crying too much?"

I told him, "No, it is not you. If anyone is to blame, it would be me because I cried the loudest." I assured him, "You have always been a good boy." And I promised him I would always be here to protect him.

I guess that was all I could do. The crying went on for countless nights. Over time, I guess we both realized that crying did not help, so we stopped. Maybe we simply learned to accept the reality and need to live with it.

One morning about one month after Mom's departure, we suddenly found out that our Uncle Teng had run away. We found a note on his bed that said, "Sorry, Mom and Dad. My friends and I decided to join the Khmer Rouge. Please don't worry. I will come back soon."

After reading the note, Grandma sobbed, "I don't understand this. I thought he was happy. Why did he do this?"

Grandpa read the note and quickly lit a match to burn it. He asked everyone to come inside the house. He closed the door and said, "Look, nobody outside this house needs to know this. If a neighbor or friend asks how Teng is or where he went, we all must reply with the same answer. And the answer must be that Teng has moved to work in Phnom Penh and that he is good and well."

Grandpa asked the questions and made each of us reply, rehearsing to ensure we got it. One by one, we said, "Teng has moved to work in Phnom Penh."

We never mentioned Uncle Teng's name again. In fact, my parents' situation was also never brought up in daily conversation. We really did not know where my parents went. We just assumed they also joined the Khmer Rouge. You see, this was wartime. It would be extremely dangerous for any family living in the city to have family members known to join the Khmer Rouge. For the safety of everyone, Grandpa wanted to make sure we got this: nobody outside this household (no cousin, neighbor, or friend) could know about this.

Soon it was time for me to attend school. But my younger brother was still one year away from school age. Each morning Grandma would walk me to school. While my brother still stayed at home, I snuck out and ran home during break time after my first class to check on him.

The teacher tried to stop me from running home. A teacher would keep me in the classroom during break time and personally hand me over to the next class. But I had no interest in the next class. All I could think of was getting to my younger brother back home. I would cry and fight off anything that stopped me from going home.

This went on for a couple days. Grandma later told me the school principal asked her to come to school for a meeting. As many parents know, normally this is not good. Grandma learned of the school dilemma. Grandma told the school principal that we had recently became orphaned. The school principal felt sorry for us, I guess, and told her, "Maybe it is better to enroll them together when the young one is ready."

We went back to school again a year later, this time with my brother in the same classroom, and we were good and happy. Looking back, many people at the school thought we were the odd twins because we do not look alike. I mean, we look like brothers for sure. But we do not look like most twins.

We finally settled in and lived in Kampot with our maternal grandparents plus a few uncles and aunts. Kampot is a coastal city located in the southern part of Cambodia, and it borders South Vietnam. Kampot was divided into north and south by a river, the main city market on the north and the city outskirts in the south. There were two main bridges in Kampot, a bridge for trains on the west side and a road bridge on the east side. The two bridges were approximately two kilometers apart. And Grandma's house was situated just about halfway between the two.

Grandma had a big house, at least three thousand square feet, and it sat on a big piece of property in Kampot prime location. Her property was surrounded by coconut trees in the front, banana trees on the left, and mango and other tropical trees on the right. There was plenty of room for her five children, who were living at home at the time, plus my brother and I to roam around. She also raised chickens, ducks, four dogs, and a half-dozen pigs.

Grandpa worked in Kampot. He rode a bike to work every morning and returned home every afternoon. I was told he was an accounting manager at a trading company. He was good at what he did, and he was well-known in the industry.

One day he returned home and told Grandma excitedly, "I got a good job offer, and the position will be in Phnom Penh. I can go there first. Once I settle in, I can bring you and the kids to Phnom Penh." He added, "The fighting is getting closer and closer to Kampot. Phnom Penh will be a safer place for us."

He accepted the job and moved to Phnom Penh by himself first, while Grandma and the children stayed in Kampot. Grandpa would come home maybe once a month for a weekend. I always looked forward to seeing Grandpa come home, as Grandma would cook his favorite dishes and we had plenty to eat. Plus sometimes Grandpa brought us new toys from Phnom Penh.

My grandma frequently walked to Kampot market to buy fresh vegetables, pork, and groceries. Sometimes she asked me to come along. The market center was about three kilometers away from Grandma's place. From her house, we would turn right and walk along the road, heading to the road bridge, for about a kilometer.

We would then turn left to walk onto the bridge and continue to walk across it. Once we crossed the bridge, we would continue to head north for four blocks to get to the market center. After the grocery shopping, we would return home, taking a ride on a tricycle because we had many bags to carry.

From Grandma's house, you could simply walk across a quiet road, and in five minutes, you would be at the riverbank. The road in front of Grandma's house hardly had any cars because there was a newer road just completed not too long ago and most of the car traffic had been diverted there.

The river was beautiful and had plenty of fish. Cambodia is a tropical country. There are mainly two seasons, rain and dry. During the rainy season, we would catch freshwater fish. During the dry season, the freshwater retreats, and the river would be filled in by high tide with seawater. The fish we caught this time would be sea fish.

By 1971, the government forces only controlled about twenty kilometers within the Kampot radius. The Khmer Rouge occupied the territory outside the radius. Military stations or checkpoints would mark the territory at all roads entering the city.

Between 1970 to 1972, life in Kampot was frequently disrupted by bomb explosions in the market or a surprise attack on city police stations or any government buildings. The school class was no exception. I remembered we would hear a loud explosion in a distance at night, and the next day there would be no school.

But I did not worry or have any concerns. I had plenty of fun things to do. My brother and I would go out to fish along the riverbank, or sometimes we wandered out further to fish along the seashore. We caught many varieties of fish, shrimp, crab, and sea snail and brought them home. Grandma would happily prepare and cook our fresh catch.

From Grandma's house, if I turned left and walked toward the railroad, I would find rice paddy fields on both sides of the road. The rice fields in Cambodia mostly are constructed in square, rectangular, or triangle shapes, depending on the property line. Each rice field is surrounded by levies about knee high and one meter wide for a man to walk on it.

Rice planting needed a lot of water. The rice field would normally be filled with water up to knee-high for about three months by Mother Nature or an irrigation canal. During this period, the rice field would have many mosquitoes and small insects. The mosquitoes and insects were naturally a source of food for crabs, frogs, and fish.

After rice harvesting season, the rice field would become dry. When we walked in the rice field right after the harvest, we would often find holes, typically arm-length deep, along the levee walls. Crabs created these holes. But you would find it was home to an odd couple, a crab and a frog together.

You see, the crabs were afraid of the mosquitoes because the mosquito would bite their eyes. And the frogs ate the mosquitoes. When both residents were home and a mosquito came in, the crab would retreat to hide behind the frog. The frog would jump out to eat the mosquito, and the crab was protected. In return, if the intruder happened to be a snake, the crab would move to the front to fight off the snake, and the frog would be safely protected behind the crab. Isn't it amazing how nature works?

The best time to catch crabs and frogs was after the rice harvest. This was because they had been well-fed and tasty. To catch crab and frog, we only needed two things, a one-meter stick with a hook at one end and a bag made of cloth with a string we could pull and close quickly. A stick was used to survey what was in the hole. When I used a stick to poke into the hole, I would try to feel. Was it hard or soft?

If I reached in and felt something hard, very likely it was a crab. I would use the hook to pull out the crab, catch it, and drop it in a bag. After catching the crab, I would use my hand to reach into the hole to catch the frog. And sure enough, 90 percent of the time I would find a frog behind the crab.

Warning! Do not put your hand in a hole if it is soft. If you feel something soft in the hole before you pull out a crab, this means it is highly likely a snake is inside. The snake must have come in while the crab was out hunting for food. No one was around to protect the frog. The snake had swallowed the frog and was now resting inside the hole. When I suspected a snake was inside, I would leave it alone and move on to the next hole.

Back to Grandma's house in Kampot. One night, a big and very loud explosion woke us up. The noise was so loud that it shook the ground like a big earthquake. But Kampot region is not in a earthquake zone. We woke up and ran outside the house to see what was going on. We saw big smoke about a kilometer away or in the direction of the road bridge.

By sunlight, we finally realized the explosion had completely blown away the middle section of the bridge. There was no doubt this explosion was the work of the Khmer Rouge. Overnight, we and other residents on this side of the river were cut off from Kampot. People quickly needed to find a way to get to and from the Kampot market. Within days, Kampot ingenuity kicked in. Local fishing boats of all sizes were turned into floating taxis, taking people across the river.

By early 1973, the Khmer Rouge gained more ground, and the fighting was getting closer and closer, now approximately ten kilometers outside Kampot. During the day, we would see a strange-looking plane. The front half was a cockpit, and the second half had a hollow square shape. The plane would be circling high above the air in the distance not too far. I was told this was a US spy plane running reconnaissance operations above the Khmer Rouge control region.

By night, we would hear military helicopters flying in the same areas, as if the spy plane found something. As the helicopters circled above, we would see flashes of gunfire shooting down for about ten to twenty minutes before the helicopters flew away. As the fighting intensified and got closer each day, Grandpa decided to move the family to Phnom Penh to be in a safer place.

Phnom Penh is a capital city and the biggest city in Cambodia. There were a lot of buildings and many more people. Phnom Penh population was about 2 million in 1973, a 50 percent increase compared to a year ago. Many people were coming in from other cities as the Khmer Rouge force moved closer to capture more cities.

Grandpa rented a sizeable place for the family, a total of ten people, near the city center. I cannot remember the exact street name. I looked at Google Maps. It should be along Kampuchea Krom Boulevard and near the junction of street 169. I recognized this based on three Phnom Penh landmarks: the National Olympic Stadium, the Phnom Penh New Market, and Sihanouk Hospital Center of Hope.

This was the main road from Phnom Penh Central Market to the international airport. The airport was about fifteen kilometers from the New Central market. Our house was about one-and-a-half kilometers from the New Central market. I recalled walking there quite often. Many buildings on both sides of Kampuchea Krom Boulevard were three or four stories. This was one of the bustling areas of Phnom Penh in 1973.

The ground floor was mostly occupied by stores and businesses of all kinds (restaurants, motorbike shops, grocery stores, tailor shops, jewelry stores, bakeries, and cafés). The upper floors mostly were residential. We occupied the whole second floor. This was considered a large place based on local standards. Not many families could afford a whole floor at the time.

The whole family, ten people, were now living in Phnom Penh. I learned Grandpa was a senior manager working for an airline company called Air Cambodia. No wonder Grandpa could afford to rent such a big place in Phnom Penh.

Air Cambodia was providing passenger and cargo services between different cities across Cambodia. This was the only mode of transportation since all roads between cities were cut off due to the civil war. I assume it was a very lucrative business.

Living in Phnom Penh was very exciting for me. To me, this was a new frontier, with so many new things and places to explore. We enrolled at a local school not too far, and we only had class for half a day. I was now about nine years old and learned I could get into a movie theater free with an accompanied adult ticket. I would go to a movie theater after school and wait for an adult stranger who bought a ticket. When they were walking to the ticket checkpoint to enter the theater, I would sneak closer to them as if I was their kid.

Half the time, I made it in to see a movie for free, mostly Hong Kong kung fu movies starring Bruce Lee and others. Occasionally I saw some French movies with subtitles. There was no Hollywood movie on the big screen in Phnom Penh in the 1970s. At least I could not recall it.

After a while, I also learned a way to make some money. I would save some pocket money every day. After a few weeks, I got enough money to buy a few cartoon books. I would bring them to the front of the school during break time. When the kids would come out to buy some snacks and drinks, I would display my cartoon book collection for rent, side by side with other vendors. Some kids would rent my books to read or look at pictures for a small fee. The kids would return the book when the school bell rang, and I would return home.

This turned out to be quite a lucrative business for me at the time. Within weeks, I got more money to buy more books, and my book renting business grew. There were too many books for me to carry by myself, so I hired my brother to help out.

Soon a new year arrived. It was now 1975, and the news of Khmer Rouge attacks filled the front page of daily papers. There was a hospital one block behind our house (I believe this hospital is now called Sihanouk Hospital Center of Hope), and inside the hospital, there used to be a big field, now turned into a helicopter landing spot. We could see helicopters landing and taking off many times a day. The wind and noise were so bad. This is why I could still vividly recall it.

The helicopters brought in the injured people. I was told most of the injured were soldiers from the front line. Sometimes civilians were also injured when they were in the wrong place at the wrong time.

Two

Khmer Rouge Victory and Forced Evacuation

April 14 is a Cambodian New Year Day. Normally Phnom Penh streets would be full of people celebrating this annual and traditional festival. One distinctive feature for this celebration was street gambling. Gambling would be legal in many cities across Cambodia for three days during New Year festivities. All kinds of street vendors would set up tents and gambling tables along the sidewalks. Everyone would come out to celebrate and place their bets, legally, during this traditional holiday.

But in early April 1975, Phnom Penh city was unusually quiet and very tense. Most people stayed home. Many stores and offices in the city were closed. Only a few essential stores, bakeries, and groceries were still open. This was because the Khmer Rouge had intensified their attack on Phnom Penh in the past two weeks, and the sounds of gunfire and rockets were getting louder and more frequent.

The Khmer Rouge was advancing closer and closer to the city from all four directions. By 9:00 a.m. on April 14, 1975, the Khmer Rouge force finally captured the Phnom Penh radio station. We could hear on the radio as the Khmer Rouge announced the victory. The broadcast played the Khmer Rouge national anthem, and they urged the last few soldiers from the former regime to surrender.

After hearing the victory news on the radio, we were all very happy to hear the civil war had ended. I guess many people had enough of the fighting and many refugees in Phnom Penh could not wait to go back to their home city and start a normal life again. We looked out onto Kampuchea Krom Boulevard from our second-floor balcony. We still could not see any sign of Khmer Rouge soldiers. But we saw some Lon-Noh soldiers running north toward the central market. We saw a few Lon-Noh soldiers run into the alley between buildings. They went in, and a few minutes later they came out in civilian clothes. They had abandoned their uniforms and guns and run away on foot, like a dog running away with its tail tucked in when it got scared.

Soon we heard a few gunshots from a distance. We all ducked down and away from the balcony. Then we heard people chanting, "The war is over! Long live Cambodia!"

We stood up cautiously and looked onto the street below again. This time we saw a hundred-plus Khmer Rouge soldiers in small groups of five or six. Most were marching in on foot, but some on bicycles and a few on motorbikes. Joining them a few minutes later, we saw a handful of Khmer Rouge drive in on a jeep.

Normally retreating soldiers would burn or destroy their gear, rockets, ammunition, tanks, trucks, and jeeps before they were abandoned. This would not allow the enemy to use it. Almost all Lon-Noh soldiers were using American guns and gear. The jeep must have been abandoned by the Lon-Noh soldiers in panic and they had no time to destroy it. We assumed the Khmer Rouge on the jeep were the leaders, as the Khmer Rouge uniform did not show their rank. (The Khmer Rouge uniform is black khaki Mao shirt, Mao pants, and Mao cap. Mao refers to Mao Ze Dong, a Chinese communist leader.)

Many people came out onto the street to celebrate the Khmer Rouge victory. Some people handed out water, Pepsi, and food to the Khmer Rouge soldiers. We could tell these Khmer Rouge soldiers had never drank a Pepsi. One drank it quickly, as if it were water and choked. A few Khmer Rouge soldiers thought the Pepsi was poisonous. They quickly pointed their AK-47s at a man and a woman who had just handed out Pepsi.

"What drink is this? You tried to poison us!"

The man quickly said, "No, sir. It is a very good drink for a hot day."

The woman hurriedly opened her bottle, drank it, and added, "Sir, it is not poisonous. I drink it too. Everybody loves it."

The Khmer Rouge paused and was still not sure what to believe. Another man from the back row jumped to the front.

He opened a new bottle of Pepsi, drank it, and said, "Look, sir, it is really not poisonous."

The crowd also joined in, "It is not poisonous. We all drink it every day."

The Khmer Rouge now looked relaxed. He took another shot and choked again.

A man quickly showed him how to drink Pepsi. "Take a small sip, but don't take too much each time."

Another Khmer Rouge soldier followed the man's instruction. He took a small sip, and this time he did not choke.

Other Khmer Rouge soldiers followed and said, "This is really a good drink!"

And everyone had a good laugh. One Khmer Rouge soldier noticed the people greeted them as "Sir." He told the crowd, "All Cambodians are liberated now! Ongka said we are all equal. No rich people and no poor people! No landlord oppressing poor people."

Ongka means a political party in the Cambodian language, and the Khmer Rouge used the word Ongka as Cambodian communist party.

A man from the crowd inquired curiously, "What can we call you?"

The Khmer Rouge soldier replied without hesitation, "We are all comrade. You may call me comrade. You can also call your friend comrade."

The crowd joined in loudly, "Long live comrade!"

Everyone on the street was very excited to see the end of a civil war. People were cheering, celebrating the victory by handing out beer and drinks to strangers and giving toasts to one another.

"The war is over!"

People believed life could now go back to normal, and all Cambodians could have a bright future. The victory celebration went on all day and all night on April 14, 1975, along Kampuchea Krom Boulevard, across the capital city, Phnom Penh, and all over Cambodia.

The next morning, we woke up. Many people were still in a celebratory mood. Some were still hungover, recovering from last night's celebration. We still could hear gunfire occasionally on April 15, but this time people did not mind because it was celebration gunfire aimed in the air. The day went by quickly.

The next morning, now April 16, 1975, about 10:00 a.m., we saw the Khmer Rouge soldiers driving a jeep along Kampuchea Krom Boulevard making announcements through a handheld microphone. "Dear fellow citizens, we are expecting the American plane to come and bomb our cities in the next few days. For your safety, Ongka asks everyone to evacuate the city immediately."

We heard the announcement as the Khmer Rouge jeep drove past our house along Kampuchea Krom Boulevard. We all looked at each other, confused.

Grandpa could not believe what he had just heard, so he asked, trying to reconfirm, "Did they ask us to leave our house now?"

Uncle Chin replied, "I heard the same thing."

Grandma joined in worriedly, "Where can we go? There is no taxi and no bus. Everyone is still off celebrating, and we have not packed yet." He then told the family, "Let us wait and see. I will go and talk to our neighbors. You kids please stay home and don't go out, please."

Ten of us were staying in the house at the time: Grandpa, early fifties; Grandma, early fifties; Uncle Chin, mid twenties; Aunt Lim, early twenties; Uncle Hoang, teenager; Aunt Ou, eleven years old; Aunt Leng, ten years old; me, ten years old;

my brother, Long, nine years old; and Uncle Khieng, eight years old.

About thirty minutes later, another group of Khmer Rouge soldiers drove by and made a similar announcement. "The American plane will come soon. Please leave your house immediately. You don't need to bring too much stuff. Once it is safe, you will return home within a week, tops."

Throughout the day, we heard similar messages delivered over and over again every so often by different groups of Khmer Rouge soldiers. We looked out over the second-floor balcony occasionally to gauge the situation. By noon, we began to see some families starting to evacuate. They were walking from the city center and heading south. They walked in groups of two, four, five, or ten, depending on the family size. Many people walked with a cloth bag or a bag pack. Some carried their loads over their shoulder. A few walked and pushed a bike carrying whatever they decided to bring along. A handful rode motorbikes loaded with their belongings tied to the back seat.

Now it was about 2:00 p.m. Grandpa returned and said, "Let's have lunch. After lunch, let's start to pack some clothes and food to last a few days."

We ate our lunch. Most of us did not eat much because of the anxiety. Grandma and Aunt Lim started to pack some clothes (three pairs per person), some rice and dried food, a couple of pots for cooking, and a few valuables like cash and jewelry. In the last couple of years, Cambodia had very high inflation. Many locals converted most of their cash into US dollars or bought gold bars or gold jewelry. We were no exception. Grandma loved to buy gold jewelry. She packed and hid them securely in the bags and along the seams of some of our shirts and pants.

Soon night fell. Grandpa asked everyone to gather around and said, "Look, we should all go to sleep early tonight. We may need to evacuate tomorrow. I heard people say the Khmer Rouge started checking door to door and made everyone leave, no exception."

We went to bed early that night. The next morning after breakfast, we looked out from our second-floor balcony. We saw more and more people evacuating. We heard people were leaving the city in all directions: east, west, north, and south. All the roads heading out of Phnom Penh were jammed and packed for many miles with people, bicycles, motorbikes, and cars.

No matter which way you were heading out (north, south, east, or west), it was one-way traffic. The Khmer Rouge soldiers would stop anybody who was trying to walk back into the city center. We saw a young woman in her twenties was walking past our house toward the city center. Soon a Khmer Rouge soldier stopped and asked her to go the other way.

She explained, "I came to my friend's house to celebrate the end of the war last night. My house and my family are on the east side of the city. I need to go back home to my family."

The Khmer Rouge soldier asked her not to walk toward the city. The young woman tried to run away by snaking through the crowd. The Khmer Rouge soldier fired several rounds in the air with his AK-47. Everyone crouched down and shook frightfully.

The Khmer Rouge soldier warned the young woman, "Do not go that way. Next time I will not shoot in the air."

The young woman had no choice. She turned around to join the crowd. I hope she was able to reunite with her family later somehow.

By 9:00 a.m., we had made our way down to the street and started walking south along Kampuchea Krom Boulevard toward the international airport. Other than Uncle Chin and Uncle Hoang, each of us carried a bag pack, each weighing about ten to fifteen pounds over the shoulder.

Grandpa told us to stick together. He also set up a system for us to stay together. I assumed Grandpa had experienced managing his airline business operation with many employees. So he knew how quickly things can get out of control if you don't have a system for everyone to follow.

The system: Uncle Hoang pushed his bike, leading the way. Grandpa would walk alongside him. The five kids walked behind Grandpa, followed by Aunt Lim and Grandma. At the tail end, Uncle Chin, with his motorbike, also carried heavy items on the back seat. Frequently Grandpa would call out one kid's name each time randomly to check.

Each one would respond, "Yes, sir."

Sometimes he would call out, "Check if Chin is still at the back."

We would turn around, check, and reply, "Yes."

Some people were pushing a wheelchair with an elder family member or a family member with disability. Many people carried a toddler or baby on their back. A few walked with a backpack over their shoulder and one arm holding a pet (a puppy or cat). The road was noisy and chaotic.

We heard a mom calling out, "Let's go, kid. We are behind. We need to catch up to your dad or brother."

We also heard people searching for missing persons. "Heng, do you hear me?" or "Sir, have you seen my son or daughter or mom or dad?"

We had walked for about two hours now and only made about four kilometers. An average person can walk four kilometers per hour. The road was packed with people heading south. We were now reaching the outskirts of Phnom Penh and began to see some paddy fields and farmhouses.

Many Cambodian farmhouses were about 1,000 to 1,200 square feet. The roof and wall were typically built using palm leaves because palm trees were plentiful and could be found everywhere across the Cambodian landscape. The floor was built using plywood, and it normally was elevated about ten feet above ground because they kept their cattle on the ground floor. Cattle were essential livestock for many farmers in Cambodia as the cattle could help the farmers to cultivate the paddy fields. The cattle were also used to pull ox carts, a key transportation vehicle in rural Cambodia.

It was now about noon. Grandpa spotted an abandoned farmhouse just off the road, a sign of abandoned house as it had no roof. We saw a few families resting there. They looked like us, just evacuated from Phnom Penh. Uncle Chin found a vacant spot under a big tree at the back of the property. We decided to stop and rest there.

In 1975, rural Cambodia farmhouses did not have running water. There were also no 7-Elevens or any convenience stores. Fortunately, all farmhouses had a water well. We brought a bucket and rope. Uncle Hoang scooped up drinking water from the well. It was not as good as a can of cold beer or soda, but it still tasted refreshingly good.

We rested for an hour and started walking again. We saw many more rice paddy fields on both sides of the road as we moved further away from Phnom Penh. Normally the rice paddy fields are green and beautiful, per my recollection when we were at Grandma's house back in Kampot. But what we saw this time was shockingly different. We saw smoke and fire burning here and there across the field. We spotted many dead soldiers also scattered across the field, some facedown and others face-up. From their uniform, we could tell which side they were on. The bodies appeared to still be fresh. They must have recently become the casualty of fighting in the last few days before the war ended. So sad.

Grandpa tried to speed up and ask us to catch up as if he did not want us, the five kids, to see too much of the war casualties. Along the road, we saw more farmhouses on both sides of the road. The houses were about five hundred meters apart with rice paddy fields between them. Some farmhouses were burned to the ground, maybe hit by a rocket. Other houses stayed untouched, but with no residents. Some houses had no roofs left. The only wall still standing looked like it had been abandoned for some time.

Now it was about 4:00 p.m. We had walked past Phnom Penh international airport. We were now about twenty kilometers from Phnom Penh.

Grandpa said, "Let's find a place to sleep tonight."

In Cambodia, sunset is around 7:00 p.m. And in war-torn Cambodia in 1975, there was no motel or hotel and restaurant in sight. We must find a spot to cook meals, shower, and sleep for ten people. We spotted a farm property not too far from the road. Grandpa sent Uncle Hoang to check it out.

I asked, "Can I go with him?"

Grandma nodded, and we went.

The farmhouse had been abandoned for some time. Half of the roof was open, and spider webs were everywhere. My uncle and I climbed up the wooden step to the elevated floor to check it out. It might have been abandoned because the owner moved away or had been killed during the war. There was no sign of recent life in the house, no usable household items like pots, cups, clothing, and so forth. Dust, leaves, and spider webs covered most of the surface. We found half the floor still had a roof.

Uncle Hoang turned to me. "This is not Holiday Inn, but I think we can find a place to rest here tonight. What do you think?"

Just kidding. No, he did not say that. He looked at me and asked, "This house still has a roof. We could sleep here, right?"

I turned to him and replied worriedly, "Really? The floor is so dirty. How can we sleep here?"

He said apologetically, "I know, but we have been walking all day. And it will get dark soon. Go and ask Grandpa to come and take a look."

I ran out to get Grandpa. "Please come and take a look."

Grandpa came, looked at the place, and said, "Let's rest here tonight before other people crowd this place."

Grandma and the party moved in. We all looked disgusted with the place, but we were too exhausted to complain.

Grandpa put on his managerial cap and started to assign duties to everyone. "Hoang, you go fetch some water. Chin, you go to check out if there are farmers nearby and see if you can buy chicken or some vegetables. Minh, Long, and Khieng, you three go to find some dead wood to burn for cooking. Grandma and Aunts, sweep and clean up the floor and prepare dinner."

Uncle Chin returned about an hour later with three live chickens. Apparently he walked to a farmhouse about two kilometers from here and had paid three times the market price. We did not care. We were grateful we got chicken for dinner tonight. Before sunset, other families also decided to find vacant spots on the same property to rest. We did not mind that they decided to join us. In fact, we felt safer to have some company. Soon it was dark, and we went to bed.

The next day after breakfast, Grandpa said, "Let's stay here for a couple of days. This place is not bad, right? Plus, we will go back to Phnom Penh in a few days."

We all nodded, and Grandpa continued, "Chin, please go out and see if they are starting to allow people to go back to Phnom Penh. The rest of you, do not wander far."

Throughout the morning, we continued to see people walking from the city and heading south. About 11:00 a.m., a group of soldiers with AK-47s walked toward us at the farmhouse.

The Khmer Rouge soldier asked, "Are you guys heading out soon?"

Grandma replied, "No, we planned to stay here for a day or two. Once they let people go back to Phnom Penh, we will be heading home."

The Khmer Rouge answered, "No, you cannot stay here. You need to move south like those people."

Grandpa assured the Khmer Rouge, "Yes, we will be on our way after lunch." He then turned to Uncle Hoang. "Go to the roadside to find Chin and ask him to come back now."

We had a quick lunch and were back on the road, heading south again. Each person carried a bag pack. Uncle Hoang pushed his bike with a rolled mat and a bigger bag filled with bedsheets. Uncle Chin pushed his motorbike with a heavier load.

Along the road, we saw a man try to empty his motorbike gas tank. This looked very strange.

Uncle Chin inquired casually, "Is it too heavy and you tried to make it lighter?"

The man replied softly "No, I heard the Khmer Rouge soldiers started demanding people give away their motorbike. And if you refused, they will not be happy. These Khmer Rouge had guns. If they want your bike, there is nothing you can do to stop them. But I assume without gas they probably don't want it."

Uncle Chin paused and then continued walking. About an hour later, we actually saw a Khmer Rouge soldier take a motorbike away from a man. And the Khmer Rouge soldier rode the bike away cheerily, like a boy who had just gotten a new toy. The man, the motorbike owner, was shocked that he was robbed of his bike by an authority in broad daylight.

Uncle Chin soon moved to the roadside, stopped, and unloaded his baggage to the ground. He emptied his gas tank, and we continued walking south. We walked for another ten kilometers that afternoon. We were now about thirty kilometers from Phnom Penh. We found a place along the road to rest for the night. The Khmer Rouge made us move every day, heading south.

Now it was day five, or April 19, 1975. While we were having breakfast, Grandma informed us worriedly, "We only have food to cover one more day."

Grandpa told Uncle Chin to go and check if we could buy some rice and food. Uncle Chin went out and returned empty-handed this time. He looked sad as he was walking back.

Grandpa noticed something was not right and asked, "What happened? Were you not able to buy stuff?"

Uncle Chin replied, "We cannot use the money anymore."

Grandma inquired curiously, "Why? If we cannot use the money, how are we going to buy food?"

Grandpa tried to calm everyone down. "Maybe we have a new currency. Don't panic just yet. Let's wait and see how we can exchange the new currency with old notes."

Uncle Chin replied, "I am not sure about the new currency. But the Khmer Rouge soldier told me if we continue to head south, they have stations giving out rice and food."

We packed up and continued walking south along National Highway 3. We walked some five kilometers and saw a group of people queuing for something at a farmhouse. We went in to check, and sure enough, a few Khmer Rouge soldiers were distributing rice and food. We joined the queue and got to the end about ten minutes later.

A Khmer Rouge soldier sitting on a chair next to a desk asked, "Family name? And how many people?"

Uncle Chin pointed to us and said, "Chin Ly and ten people."

The Khmer Rouge soldier said, "Forty bowls for the Ly family. This should last four days."

A second Khmer Rouge scooped up forty bowls of rice and poured them into our rice sack, and another Khmer Rouge handed us some dried fish.

A bowl was made of half a coconut shelf. In rural Cambodia, people made use of whatever resources Mother Nature provided. The coconut tree produced fruit. Juice could make cooking oil and soap. The coconut shelf was frequently used as a container. Palm trees produced fruit and juice. The juice could turn into sugar. Palm leaves could be used for roofs and walls. You now can see coconut trees and palm trees are an essential part of Cambodian lives.

After getting our food supply, we continued to walk south. We needed to keep walking. Each day we were drifting further and further away from Phnom Penh. Each night we spent the night along the roadside and hoped that the next morning we would be told, "You can go back home now." But that news never came.

Now it was day nine. At midday, we took a short rest on the roadside under a tree. Another family was also resting at a spot near us.

Grandpa walked over and asked a man, "Sir, I heard we can no longer use the old notes. Do you know where can we exchange for a new currency?"

The man shook his head. "No new currency I was told yesterday. In this new society, we will not need any money." The new society referred to the new Khmer Rouge regime.

Grandpa was confused. "Did you say we will not need money?"

The man replied, "Yes, the Khmer Rouge told me. Under the new society, Ongka will provide food and other stuff to everyone equally. No more need for money."

We were all very confused and had many questions. When could we go back home? Would my job still be there for me? If we could not go back to the old job, what jobs were available? And without money, how would we get paid?

Unfortunately there was nobody we could ask to get clarification. Although Grandpa did not say much, I could tell he started to worry. Anyway, we packed up and said goodbye to the family. We continued our walk heading south. Soon we saw people queuing for something. We thought this was another Khmer Rouge food distribution post.

We went in and hoped to restock our supply. There were three groups of Khmer Rouge men. Each group had two people, and they did not look like Khmer Rouge soldiers as they carried no gun and they were older men in their forties.

One of the Khmer Rouge men approached us and explained the process, "You can get some supply based on your family size. After collecting your food, you may either go with the men from group A or group B or continue your journey wherever you want to go. For group A, these men will bring you to settle in a village about five kilometers to the left from here. For group B, these men will bring you to settle in another village seven kilometers to the right from here. Once you get to the village, Ongka will arrange housing for your family. Ongka will also arrange work for each of you."

Uncle Chin acknowledged and replied, "Chin Ly, ten people, and we will continue southward."

After getting our food supply, we continued southward. We walked until about noon and stopped for a rest. Grandpa now prepared to accept the new reality that we would not be able to go back to Phnom Penh.

He calmly said, "Look, you all heard the man. We might not be able to go back to Phnom Penh. If we need to start a new life somewhere, Kampot region would be our best bet.

We don't know anything around here. But we know Kampot region well. We should be fine in Kampot."

Grandma agreed, "Let's go back home to Kampot." Kampot was still ninety kilometers from here.

Let me pause for a moment and run a recap for you. I want to make sure you understand the full magnitude and its implication of what had just happened. It was only ten days since the war ended. The Khmer Rouge forcefully evacuated millions of city dwellers from every city across Cambodia to leave their home in a hurry without any preparation. We were deceitfully told that American planes would come to bomb the cities and this evacuation was for our safety. Everyone left behind everything at home in the city and came out with only a bag pack over their shoulder. We were assured that we would be returning home in just a few days. Now we learned that not only could we not return to our home but also our money, no matter how much we brought out or left behind, was now worthless. Yes, it was nada.

To the Khmer Rouge leadership who schemed up and rolled out this deceitful plan, they might consider this was a great success, a perfect plan and flawlessly executed. They obviously did not care about the human cost at all.

But to the millions of Cambodian ordinary city dwellers, like Grandpa and Grandma, this new reality was surely devastating. To this day, I still could not comprehend how Grandpa and Grandma survived such a monumental blow. Grandpa and Grandma had been working very hard all their lives to support the family. They finally built up enough savings and would be retiring comfortably within five to ten years. Now in their fifties, without any warning, they were told that not only had all their wealth been turned to zero, but that they would also need to start a new life. They had no idea or any control over what would be happening to them and their families in this new society. What job would they get? Where would they stay? Would the children be able to continue schooling?

Three

The Cement Factory

Let's get back to the road. We had been walking south for fifteen days now, since we had left Phnom Penh. We had walked for some 120 kilometers. After another twenty kilometers, we would reach Kampot.

We arrived at a small town. I did not know the official name of the town. I simply called it Cement Factory because a cement factory was nearby. We were planning to continue walking to Kampot, but a barricade blocked the road.

A couple of Khmer Rouge soldiers came out and asked, "Where are you planning to go? You cannot continue southward."

Uncle Chin replied, "We plan to go to Kampot. It is our home there."

The Khmer Rouge soldier answered, "No, you cannot go to Kampot. Nobody can go to Kampot."

Uncle Chin explained, "We have a fruit farm on the south side of Kampot. Can we walk past Kampot and go to our farm?"

The Khmer Rouge replied, "No, nobody can go past this point without paper."

Uncle Chin asked, "Where and how can we get the approval paper?"

The Khmer Rouge soldier said impatiently, "Look, you will not get any approval paper. It is four o'clock now. I suggest you find a place to rest for the night over there." He pointed to an abandoned farmhouse. "Tomorrow you go back north for two kilometers. You will see our comrade setup station under two palm trees on the right side. They will take care of you."

We had no other option but to find a place to rest for the night. The next morning, we headed back north. Sure enough, there was a Khmer Rouge post on the right and under two palm trees. There were two groups of Khmer Rouge men ready to register newcomers' names and occupations. All newcomers were assigned to group A or group B based on their occupation in the old society. Old society referred to the Lon-Noh regime prior to the Khmer Rouge victory.

Group A

For all ordinary city citizens who neither had college degrees nor were civil servants, Ongka would take us to our new home in the village. Ongka would assign us to the work group.

Group B

For educated people with college degrees or were civil servants, like teachers, doctors, and other former government employees, Ongka told them that Ongka valued their expertise and experiences; thus they would be assigned duties based on their expertise. Ongka needed them to help rebuild Cambodia.

Some four years later, after the collapse of the Khmer Rouge regime, we learned of the horrific genocide. The Khmer Rouge rounded up many educated Cambodians and killed them all within days after these patriotic people signed up, supposedly to help rebuild Cambodia. The Khmer Rouge believed these educated classes had been heavily polluted with capitalist ideology, and they did not want any of these to take root and spread in the Khmer Rouge's new society.

We were assigned to group A, thanks to Grandpa's precautious action. Grandpa and Uncle Chin registered their occupation as taxi drivers. More newcomer families showed up at this station as the day went. By noon, Ta-Heng, group A leader, got six families, or a total of fifty people. Some families came from Kampot; others came from Ta Keo, a city east of Kampot. There were two other families like us who came from Phnom Penh.

Ta-Heng gave a briefing about the village and said it was about five kilometers from here. By 2:00 p.m., Ta-Heng told us that we needed to leave now. Everyone packed up and followed Ta-Heng to the new village. We trekked past many paddy fields into the heart of rural Cambodia. Finally we got to the village at about 3:30 p.m.

We noticed many abandoned properties in this village. There must have been at least fifty families who used to live in this village when the civil war began back in 1970, based on the number of abandoned properties we saw. Now in 1975, only about thirty families remained here. What happened to those families? We did not know for certain. We could only assume some escaped to the city and never returned. Some might have been killed during the war.

Ta-Heng and his assistants each assigned two families. We followed our new comrade named Makara, who took us to a vacant property, basically an abandoned property with two big mango trees. Overgrown weeds and shrubs covered the property. We could tell there used to be a house here, as we could still see the wood post markings on the ground. Other than that, nothing else was visible.

Makara pointed and said, "Here you are, the Ly family, this is your new home. I will come and see you tomorrow."

The next morning, Comrade Makara showed up around 9:00 a.m. He asked Uncle Chin and Uncle Hoang to go with him to grab some tools we would need. They came back thirty minutes later with five hoes, four machetes, a knife, and an ax.

Makara explained today he would take Uncle Chin and Hoang to get some building materials. Once we got the materials, he would show and teach us how to build our house.

Home Depot did not exist at the village. For building materials, they went to the forest about four kilometers away to find trees that were big enough and tall enough for the post. Makara also showed us how to go and cut some palm leaves. The palm leaves, after being treated, would be knit together for roofs and walls. We also went to cut certain kinds of vines from the forest. This would be used to tie things together to build our new house. For a floor, we cut down big bamboo and split it in half.

Makara showed us the steps we needed to follow to build a house:

Step 1

We cut the tree to length, about ten or twelve feet, carried it back, and dropped it in a lake to treat for ten days. This killed insects and any termites inside the wood. The expansion and shrinking also made the post last longer.

Step2

We cut palm leaves and vines and soaked them in the lake for five days. This would make the palm leaves and vines elastically stronger.

Step 3

While the materials were being treated, we started to dig holes for each post, at least arm-length deep. We then started to split the bamboo in half and let it dry in the open air. The bamboo would be used as a floor.

Step 4

We started house construction after the second week.

We built our house in four weeks from scratch. It was quite amazing to see the house come together. We had none of the modern tools and gear—no pickup truck to haul the wood from the forest to the lake, no power saw, and no nails.

Needless to say, this took a lot of hard labor work. But I found this to be a very rewarding experience, although I was too young to do heavy work. I helped out with whatever task was within my ability. We really appreciated Makara's guidance. We were city people. We would not be able to build a house without his assistance and guidance.

We had more new city families arriving in the village daily since our arrival. The newcomers now totaled about two hundred. Now every family had a house to stay in. Ongka started to arrange people into work groups.

In theory, there should be no more class systems under the communists. Everyone was supposed to be equal. But in reality, under the Khmer Rouge, every Cambodian was assigned to one of the two classifications.

Old Comrade

Since the Khmer Rouge started its revolution against the Lon-Noh government in rural Cambodia and many rural peasants had family members joining the Khmer Rouge army, people like Ta-Heng and the twenty families remaining in this village during the civil war were granted an honorable title, "old comrade." This is a privilege class given by the Khmer Rouge, and it had many advantages.

Newcomer

The Khmer Rouge called all city dwellers "newcomers," like our family, because we were new to life in the rural areas or countryside. And newcomers were considered dispensable because we had no contribution to Ongka (i.e., we did not support Ongka during the civil war) and now Ongka believed the revolution did not need us. This segregation was based on perceived political loyalty. I used perceived political loyalty because some city people might support the Khmer Rouge during the civil war too. But that did not count since you lived in the city; you were considered procapitalist. To the Khmer Rouge, this means you were anticommunist. And the implication of this classification was huge. Every aspect of one's life in the new society would be based on which group you were assigned to. To name a few:

1. All newcomers were considered suspect enemy or counterrevolutionist.
2. Newcomers would be assigned to do more labor-intensive or less desirable work.
3. Newcomers would receive less food and food of poorer quality.
4. No newcomer could be a supervisor or get a managerial job.
5. No matter what it is, old comrades would always get priority over newcomers.

Now it was about June 1975. It was the rainy season. This was the prime time to start rice seeding and planting. Ta-Heng, with his assistants, organized the newcomers into work groups.

Men Group

Men between the ages of sixteen to forty-five were to plow the paddy field. One old comrade was assigned to supervise ten newcomers. The men would go to plow the field using mostly traditional farm tools. They would work from 8:00 a.m. to 4:00 p.m.

Women Group

Women between the age of sixteen to forty were to do rice seeding and planting. The women team were organized in similar structures and same work hours as the men group.

Senior Group

They stayed home to cook and take care of younger kids.

Youth Group

This was children from age ten to fifteen years old. Each morning, the youth members would go to class. And in the afternoon, each boy was assigned two cattle to graze. I used class, not school, because there was only one class. All thirty-plus kids of different ages from a village would sit in a class with only one teacher. The desks and bench chairs were made of bamboo. Every day, we were repeatedly brainwashed with

> Ongka led a revolution to fight foreign and capitalist oppressors; Ongka chased away foreign oppressors and its puppet government. Ongka liberated and saved all Cambodian workers and farmers. Ongka loves us, the kids, more than our parents. As we are Cambodia future, we must be loyal to Ongka. We must report all counter-revolution words or actions to Ongka.

By noon, the boys would go to the field to pick up their two cows and graze them until 5:00 p.m. You see, the rice fields in Cambodia mostly are constructed in square or rectangular shapes, depending on the property line. Each rice field is surrounded by levees about knee-high and about three feet wide. This became a walkway between paddy fields. There were many miles of walkways between the paddy fields. And there were lots of grasses on these walkways. There were also rice crops on both sides of these walkways, and the cattle loved to graze on rice crops. I guess, if grasses were a main course to the cattle, rice crops would be their dessert. We, the boys, were to stay alert and keep an eye on the cattle constantly to make sure the cattle were well-fed and didn't graze on crops.

On weekdays, each supervisor for the men group and women group would lead their team to work in the field. Some fields were close by; others were farther away. Although the work ended at 4:00 p.m., sometimes they would not get home until 5:00 or 6:00 p.m.

You probably think this is not a bad life, right? Well, let me say that this is just a warm-up.

Almost all newcomers used to live and work in the city. They never worked on a farm or had any experience doing manual work. For men, after working in the field using farm tools for a few days, blisters started to show up on their palms. Let's just say, at best, it was unpleasant. Worst, it was painful. But throughout human civilization, people had been known to be very resilient to hardship of all kinds. Within a few weeks, the men would get used to it.

Like the men, the city women had never worked in the rice fields. They used to be in nice dresses and high-heeled shoes. Now these poor women had to go into the rice fields to work, planting rice seed. To plant rice seed, the women needed to stand in filthy, knee-high mud water for many hours. Whenever there was water in the paddy field, there would also be hungry leeches, waiting for prey, in the field. Leech is one of the creatures, if not the only one, which has "multiple lives." A leech cut into half would become two leeches, and a leech cut into three would become three leeches.

Anyone who has worked in the paddy field would know that getting a leech bite while working in the field is as common as getting your feet wet standing in water. While you are standing or walking in the paddy field with water up to your knee, leeches would crawl up your leg, bite your flesh, and suck your blood until it was fully fed. The bite itself was not too painful. To men and boys, we would pull it off and kill it. To women, the consequences were much more dramatic.

When the newcomer women felt something crawling up her leg for the first time, first she would scream so loud that one could hear her a mile away. Second, she would throw away whatever was on her hands, still screaming and running to high ground. Most of the time, men and women work groups were working not too far from each other. At the beginning, some men would promptly run over to rescue, to help a woman, by pulling off the leech from her leg. After a few weeks, we could still hear women screaming occasionally. But now many women learned to pull it off on her own, an improvement. And everyone would laugh it off.

For newcomers, Ongka would distribute food, rice and salt, based on your family head count. The old comrades had their own food supply from past year crops, stored on their property. (Old comrades had plenty of food.) The food provided by Ongka was never enough. For the first few months, the food Ongka gave out for a week might last, say, four days. Newcomers had to find other ways to supplement their food supply, or people reduced what they consumed each day in order to make the food last per supply frequency.

For short-term needs, Uncle Chin used the free time in the afternoon to go out to find supplemental food supplies. He would bring a watch, necklace, or new towel to trade with some old comrade for ten kilograms of rice, grain, chicken, or whatever food that was available. If you recall, the Khmer Rouge recently abolished the use of currency. And this barter trade had to be done discreetly because, if caught, we would be in big trouble. (You will see examples of trouble later.)

In addition, the younger kids like me, my brother, or my younger Uncle Khieng would go fishing, catching fish, crabs, and frogs in nearby lakes, rivers, or paddy fields. The fishing experiences we had back at my grandparents' place in Kampot turned out to be very useful. Other newcomer kids did not have those experiences, and we would teach them how to catch fish, crabs, and frogs.

Every Saturday 10:00 a.m. to 3:00 p.m., Ta-Heng would call a meeting for the village. Every person, young and old, needed to assemble on time at a designated location. The meeting place was basically another abandoned property. It had several big fruit trees with a big canopy. Overgrown weeds and shrubs covered the place. A few days before, Ta-Heng had assigned a few men to clear out the weeds and shrubs. Now it became an open-air assembly point.

Ta-Heng and a handful of Khmer Rouge local leadership team would take turns to speak. The themes of this weekly ritual typically went like this:

> "Good morning, everyone. Today our comrades and I want to cover a few items.
>
> a. The work we completed, number of acres of field we plowed in the past week, or the number of acres of forest we cleared to plant sweet corn this week
> b. What new job is in planning

c. And some propaganda: We defeated and chased away the capitalist America and its puppet government. Every Cambodian has been liberated. We forever owe this gratitude to Ongka leadership. Blah, blah, blah. Ongka told us, "We must not be afraid of hard work and sacrifice. We must trust Ongka. Ongka will lead us to a bright future."

d. Ongka also reminded all the newcomers, "You must forget and get rid of any capitalist thinking you inherited from the old society. There were still enemies hidden among us (referring to the newcomers). Ongka has eyes and ears everywhere. Ongka will not tolerate any counterrevolution thinking and behavior."

After the dreadful Saturday marathon meeting, everybody finally had one day off on Sunday. The next Monday came, and a new workweek repeated.

About four weeks after we began work in the paddy fields, Ongka asked each family, one by one, to come and collect two pairs of clothes per person. **For old comrades,** each was given two pairs of brand-new black Mao shirts and black Mao pants, folded. These were the hot fashion trends during the Khmer Rouge regime. From a practical standpoint, this also made total sense. The black color made it less likely to stain while working in the field. This was especially practical as we got no soap for laundry or any cleaning at all. The loose cutting also made it more comfortable to put on.

For newcomers, we were given two pairs of used clothes. When we got to the clothes warehouse, we saw four piles of clothes laid down on a mat, unfolded. The clothes were for men, women, boys, and girls. The clothes were mostly of light color or white. They came in all sizes and 1970s styles (bell-bottom pants, regular long pants, T-shirts, long-sleeved shirt, etc.). All the clothes were used. There was no tag. I guess Ongka got them from the goodwill stores. No, just kidding. Ongka probably got these clothes from the abandoned houses and apartments in the city where people left them behind. Nevertheless, we were grateful we got additional pairs of clothes. As you recall, most of us only brought three pairs of clothes with us.

Bell-bottom pants were not designed as work pants for the paddy fields. Similarly, lighter color shirts would stain badly when one put it on and had to work in a muddy field. For practical reason, people with bell-bottom pants cut off the lower part of the pants. People with lighter clothes tried all kinds of ways to make the color darker. A newcomer learned he could dye lighter-color fabrics and make it darker by soaking it in water with a kind of wood bark. And the kind of wood could be found in nearby forests. Soon the news spread, and everybody followed with the same formula.

The people in the village had been working in the fields for a couple of months now. On one Saturday assembly, Ta-Heng and his team took turns to speak, one by one, covering the same boring topics. But to everyone's surprise, Ta-Heng called out a man's name, Chey Dora. Mr. Chey was one of the newcomers from Phnom Penh. Like everyone, he was completely caught off guard.

Ta-Heng asked him and his wife to stand up. On the spot, Ta-Heng asked, "Please tell everyone what your occupation was in the old society."

Mr. Chey paused and nervously replied, "I worked as a gardener in Phnom Penh. My wife stayed home."

Ta-Heng loudly replied with his microphone, "I know you told Ongka you worked as a gardener. But I am asking: what was your real occupation in the old society? We heard you told your wife you missed your students and the school work and she also missed her students."

Apparently Ongka had been sending agents to spy or listen to newcomer families at night, and they overheard Mr. and Mrs. Chey's conversation at night.

Mr. Chey admitted apologetically, "Yes, we both were math teachers at a high school in Phnom Penh." He quickly added, "But we never get involved in politics. We are just ordinary teachers."

The whole place, with a hundred-plus people, suddenly became so quiet that you could hear a pin drop.

Ta-Heng concluded the meeting with, "You deceived Ongka. You know Ongka has eyes and ears everywhere. I must report this to Ongka."

A few days later, we did not see the couple show up for work. In fact, they were never seen again. Frankly, at the time, we really did not know where they were taken to or what punishment they got. Soon lives in the new village had gone back to normal, and most people probably had forgotten about the Chey couple.

A few weeks went by. One day while we were having dinner at home, one of my aunts, Ou, who was about twelve, told us Ta-Heng's wife took her to Ta-Heng's home today. She added, "Ta-Heng's wife was very nice. She gave me a banana to eat. She also asked if I am Mom's own child or adopted."

If you recall, when we left Phnom Penh right after the war ended, there were ten of us. Aunt Ou was number six. My grandma adopted Aunt Ou when she was six months old. And by race, Aunt Ou is native Cambodian. But we are Chinese-born Cambodians. One can tell this clearly because her skin is of darker complexion. In the old society, hiring housekeepers were common in Phnom Penh. This naturally triggered Ongka's suspicion that Aunt Ou might be the Ly's family child housekeeper. So you know, communist ideology against all the capitalist social structure, the master versus the maid, the capitalist versus the workers. The Khmer Rouge were steadfast in this pursuit. If there were any indication she was a child housekeeper, the Ly family would be in serious trouble. By serious, I meant the whole family would be killed.

Grandpa, Grandma, and all of us suddenly paused still for a moment, as we were completely caught off guard. Then Grandpa asked her calmly, "And what did you tell her, dear?"

Aunt Ou replied, "I told her I am adopted."

Grandma chimed in, "What else did she ask?"

Aunt Ou said, "She also asked if I am asked to do all the housework at home."

Grandma inquired worriedly, "And?"

Aunt Ou replied, "I told her my sister Leng and I normally wash the dishes together. And my niece cleans up the floor."

Grandma hugged her tightly and cried, "Good girl. Mommy loves you."

All of us were so relieved and grateful. As you can see, we had our first close call.

Six months passed since we had settled in the village. The food Ongka supplied was getting much less now. A week supply now would only last three days max. Food shortages were common among newcomer families. Many newcomer families would trade their watches and gold jewelry for food with the old comrades. It was quite interesting to observe how these two groups used the watches.

When the newcomers had watches on their wrists and old comrades did not, whenever someone asked what time it was, the newcomers would look at the watch on their wrist and give a more precise time up to the minute, say, 2:15 p.m. or 3:05 p.m.

When these watches switched owners to old comrades and someone asked what time it was, now that these old comrades each had a watch on their wrists, they did not look at the watch but still looked up and gave out the approximate time based on the position of the sun and not what the watch said, say, about 10:00 a.m. or 3:00 p.m.

This was because many old comrades were rural peasants and had never had a watch. They were isolated from modern life outside for many years. And they were so used to looking at the sun to tell time. It is hard to change old habits, I guess.

Fortunately Grandma brought all her jewelry collections. We could still trade pieces of gold jewelry for some food each week. The Wongs, another newcomer family, was not as lucky. Mr. Wong had a wife and four children (two young teenage girls and two younger boys like me). My brother and I taught them how to catch crabs and frogs.

Like us, they were also facing food shortages, but their situation was much more serious. You see, the Wongs only had four watches and a big stack of US$100 bills. After a few weeks, Mr. Wong traded out all the four watches. And the stack of US$100 notes was now worth nothing. He could no longer find food for his family. One morning, his wife found he had hung himself at night under a tree behind their house. What a tragedy.

Now Uncle Chin needed to go out further and further to find old comrades with food that were willing to trade. One Saturday late afternoon, about 5:00 p.m., I saw Uncle Chin as he was walking back home at a distance. Normally he would be walking by himself. But today, I saw three Khmer Rouge soldiers walking with him, a soldier walking alongside Uncle Chin and two soldiers with AK-47s on their shoulders walking behind. I thought this was strange. I hoped he did not get into trouble during the trade.

I quickly ran into the house to tell Grandpa. I said, "Grandpa, Uncle Chin is back. But he comes with three Khmer Rouge soldiers."

Grandpa and everyone else rushed out of the house to look, worriedly. As Uncle Chin and the Khmer Rouge soldiers got closer, Uncle Chin happily called out, "Mom! Dad! Look who I came across! It is Teng! It is Teng!"

Uncle Teng ran over quickly to hug Grandma.

Grandma hugged him tightly. She cried, "Oh my boy, how are you? I have been thinking about you all the time. But we never had any news about you. I thought I had lost you."

A few minutes later, he hugged Grandpa and each one of us, one by one.

If you recall, five years ago, back in 1970, a few weeks after my mom's departure, one of my uncles ran away from home and left a note under his pillow. That was Uncle Teng. This was the joyous moment, a family reunion, we had not had for quite a while.

Grandma and my aunt prepared dinner, and we all had a big family dinner, along with the two Khmer Rouge soldiers. Uncle Teng told us he had joined the Khmer Rouge in the Kampot region. And he had been sent to the front line multiple times to attack Kampot during the war. Currently he was stationed at a military medical post about seven kilometers from here. His post was actually not too far from the Khmer Rouge barricade where they would not allow us to walk to Kampot. He said he had been looking for us along National Highway 3 in the early days after the war ended. But somehow we had missed each other until today, when he crossed paths with Uncle Chin and the two brothers recognized each other. This was amazing, wasn't it? What were the odds?

Uncle Teng and his two comrade soldiers spent the night with us. They each had a nylon hammock tied to the trees. We were told this was how Khmer Rouge soldiers slept when they were on the road.

News traveled fast in the village, even though there was no phone or internet. Somehow Ta-Heng got the news that we had visitors from the Khmer Rouge soldiers. You see, Khmer Rouge soldiers were war heroes. I guess Ta-Heng could not wait to find out why newcomers like us in his village would have war heroes as visitors. Ta-Heng showed up about 10:00 a.m. the next morning.

Grandpa came out to greet Ta-Heng. He introduced Uncle Teng to Ta-Heng, "This is my son."

From Ta-Heng's body language, we could tell he was totally shocked. He said, "Really, you never told me that you had a son in the Liberation Army."

Grandpa replied, "We also did not know until yesterday. He left home many years ago. We thought we had lost him."

Ta-Heng and Uncle Teng exchanged pleasantries. Soon Ta-Heng invited Uncle Teng and his two comrades to his house. Uncle Teng and his two comrades went. They returned later and said goodbye to us.

A few days later, Uncle Teng and his comrades returned to visit us, and they brought us some food. Our family status changed overnight. Ta-Heng and other old comrades became friendlier to us.

Uncle Teng took me to visit his station several times. It was basically a temporary clinic set up at an abandoned house. The center provided medical treatment, injections, and wound dressing to the Khmer Rouge soldiers. Thankfully, the war had ended, and I did not need to see any serious war casualties.

The Khmer Rouge soldier uniform did not have any sign to show their ranking. We never asked Uncle Teng about his rank because whenever we saw him, he always had two soldiers with him. When I visited his medical clinic, probably twenty soldiers were working at that post. And they looked like they all reported to him. I saw all of them except Uncle Teng had AK-47s. He carried a pistol. Uncle Teng continued to visit us maybe once a month. Each time he would bring some food for the family.

Now it was about December 1975. The village had just finished our first year's harvest of rice crops. Ta-Heng thanked everyone for their hard work and celebrated the successful harvest by hosting a party with a lot of food. He also increased the weekly food supply for the newcomer families.

Soon a new year arrived, 1976, at a Saturday assembly meeting. Ta-Heng announced that Ongka had a big project for our village plus other nearby villagers. Ongka wanted to build a dam at a river upstream some thirty kilometers away. This dam would enable the village to divert the water to wherever we needed for rice planting. He needed to send ten men and ten women from our village. The selected men and women would need to leave by the end of January. They would need to walk there and stay there for three to four months. Uncle Hoang and Aunt Lim were among the people who got selected to go build the dam.

A couple of weeks before the men and women had to leave to build a new dam, Ongka gave out another two pairs of clothes to each person. A man named Samuth secretly told Uncle Hoang that he suspected one of the shirts he recently collected might belong to Mr. Chey, the teacher couple taken away to see Ongka. Samuth and Uncle Hoang used to work side by side with Mr. Chey in the field. They often sat together during a lunch break.

Samuth told Uncle Hoang, "Please don't tell anyone about this. I am scared, and I don't want us to get into trouble."

Uncle Hoang replied, "No way. This is impossible. There were many shirts with the same color and pattern. Don't worry about it."

Samuth added, "If you come to my house, I can show you the shirt."

To ease Samuth's concern, Uncle Hoang replied, "Ok, I will go with you today after work."

Uncle Hoang went to Samuth's house after work. Samuth showed him the shirt. Uncle Hoang looked at it. At first look, sure the shirt was a used shirt. It had a similar pattern, color, and cut like Mr. Chey's shirt. But this could easily be another shirt Ongka pulled out from the city apartments. It might happen to look alike and be the same size. As we know, there were many similar shirts on sale in any community or city in the old society. This could not be proof the shirt was owned by Mr. Chey.

Uncle Hoang told Samuth, "It may be just a coincidence. Don't worry."

But as soon as he finished the sentence, Uncle Hoang noticed the shirt had a small burn mark on the right sleeve. He quickly took another look at it. He then looked at other parts of the shirt.

Uncle Hoang nervously threw the shirt to the ground. He turned to Samuth and said, "I think you are right. Look at the cigarette burn on the right sleeve. Do you remember when I tried to light a cigarette for him and missed? Look at the sweat stain on the collar. If this shirt were a new arrival from the city, it should not have a collar stain like this because we had soap to clean back in the city."

Samuth nervously replied, "What should I do?"

Uncle Hoang paused for a minute and answered, "We cannot tell anyone about this. You hear me?"

Uncle Hoang never told anyone about this until three years later, after the Khmer Rouge was overthrown by Vietnamese invasion in 1979.

Back to the village. Now, about March 1976, Uncle Hoang, Aunt Lim, and other young men and women had left the village and been sent to work on the new dam. And Ta-Heng started to reduce the weekly food supply to all newcomer families. This was barely three months after the village had a successful harvest. The food supply was gradually reduced each week.

By May 1976, the food shortage with newcomer families was getting worse. This was something we, the villagers, could not understand. We had plowed every square inch of the paddy field in the village. We had so much rice grain after the harvest. What happened to all our grain?

There had been speculation that the Khmer Rouge, the central government, had set targets for each province, each village, to deliver a certain percentage of their harvest to Ongka based on the population size and acres of land. In other words, this was a form of tax to the central government because the new society had no currency. Some local leaders tried to impress his boss, to boost his own performance, by delivering more crop so to exceed target quotas. These competitive, no, I should call them selfish and greedy leaders, would send off more crops to Ongka at the expense of the villagers' food supply.

Interestingly, many years later, I observed similar human greed played out in corporate America when some senior executives would cut benefits for workers in order to jack up stock price and to boost their performance. I believe in capitalism, up to a point. I also believe greed drives motivation, motivation leads to innovation, and innovation drives productivity. This drives profit, and profit is good, again up to a point.

Greed could also cause social injustice and lead to destruction if left unchecked. Luckily in America and many Western democracies, we have laws and regulations to check and protect consumers' and workers' interests, relatively speaking.

And what did Ongka, the central government, do with all the rice? During the Khmer Rouge regime, Cambodia had no currency and literally closed its door to the world. Only a handful of communist allies (like communist China,

Vietnam, and North Korea) had diplomatic relationships with the Khmer Rouge. The only country that had a long-term trade relationship with the Khmer Rouge was communist China. Rumor was that the Khmer Rouge used the stockpiles of crops to trade with communist China for more guns and ammunition.

Back to the village. Uncle Hoang and Aunt Lim had been sent away to work on the dam project for about four months now. One Sunday, Uncle Teng came to visit us. This time he told Grandpa and Grandma that he had got an Ongka approval letter for the family to be relocated to a village on the south side of Kampot. This would be closer to Grandma's durian farm, and we should be better there. He got inside information that the life of villagers was better over there and they had no food shortages. This was a huge deal to get an Ongka approval letter to relocate.

First, no newcomer would even dare to make a request for relocation because making such a request would imply you were not happy with the current Ongka arrangement. This would make Ongka unhappy. The consequence would be very serious. Nobody could afford to go there. Please forgive me for using the baseball analogy. In baseball, you have three strikes. With Ongka, you only have one strike.

Second, we could not use a family reunion to request for relocation because we had no idea where our extended family was. We had no news at all, I meant, no mail, no radio, no newspaper, and absolutely no contact with anyone outside this village except Uncle Teng. We were completely cut off from the world beyond the village. The next village was only ten kilometers away. There was absolutely no people interaction between villagers, ordinary citizens like us. We had no idea what was going on in the next village. How many people were in the next village? Did they have food supply shortages like us?

Uncle Teng would need to jump through many hoops to get this approval to relocate his family who were newcomers. We were extremely lucky and grateful to him. Grandpa and Grandma were so happy to hear the news. But the initial excitement and joy were short-lived when we realized Uncle Hoang and Aunt Lim were not home. They had both been sent away to work on the dam project.

Grandpa told Uncle Teng, "Hoang and Lim had been sent to work on a new dam project some thirty kilometers away. We cannot go without them."

Thus Uncle Teng went to see Ta-Heng and got the approval to get Uncle Hoang and Aunt Lim to return. About a week later, Uncle Hoang and Aunt Lim returned home. We then packed up and started walking toward Kampot. For the twenty-kilometer journey, we came across four checkpoints. Each time we had to show the approval letter in order to proceed. This gave me insight into how the Khmer Rouge controlled the people. By controlling the food supply, limiting people interaction, plus controlling the news, this would make it very difficult for people to organize any uprising.

When we got closer to Kampot, about a kilometer outside, there was another checkpoint, and a Khmer Rouge soldier asked us to show the approval letter. After checking the approval letter, he then directed us to go via a detour route as nobody would be allowed to pass through the Kampot center.

We followed the detour route and got to the other side of Kampot, and we walked across the main bridge. Another

Khmer Rouge soldier station on the other side of the bridge directed us to continue going straight south. If we could turn right and walk for a kilometer, we would be at my grandparents' house in Kampot. It was so close but yet unreachable.

We stopped and slept on the roadside about three kilometers south of Kampot. That night, Uncle Hoang and Aunt Lim told us that they were ecstatic when they got the news that they were both to return home tomorrow. At the time, they were told they could return home. But they did not yet know our family had got an approval letter to relocate. The fact that they were able to leave the dam construction zone was surely a true blessing.

Uncle Hoang continued, "The first week when we got to the new dam site, it was exciting because we had never seen other young people outside our village for over a year. There were at least three hundred young people, men and women, sent there to build the new dam."

This was the first time each of them was able to meet their peers from other villages. They spent the first two weeks clearing forests and building two big camps, one for women and another one for men, about five hundred meters away from each other.

After the campsites were completed, Ongka showed them the master plan. Once completed, the dam would be forty meters high, ten meters wide, and some five kilometers long. They needed to work 8:00 a.m. to 4:00 p.m. every day. They did not have any power tools, so it was hard labor work. But these young men and women were already used to labor work in the past eight months. The problem was that the food supply frequently got disrupted due to poor road conditions.

There was no paved road from the village to the dam site at all. All the food to support the three hundred-plus young people working on the dam must be carried in by men or hauled in by ox cart. Many people did not have enough to eat. Soon hungry people became weak, and weak people became sick. And there were no good sanitation systems. Many people had to drink and bathe from the same river water.

Within a month, a few people started to have fevers. Soon people got malaria. And there were no vaccines or medical care. The diseases spread quickly among the young people, and by the third month, one or two persons died every day.

It was late. We went to sleep, and thank God that all ten of us were able to leave the Cement Factory safely. The next morning, we continued walking south to the new village, our new home.

Four

Relocation

We continued to head south for another day. We finally arrived at our new village. I could not remember the name of this village, but I recalled it was about twenty kilometers south of Kampot. This was not too far from Grandma's durian fruit farm. In fact, we were walking past the road to Grandma's durian orchard. We literally saw it from a distance, yet we could not step foot on it.

The landscape in this region was quite different compared to that at the Cement Factory. Over there, we could see paddy fields everywhere you looked. Over here, we saw paddy fields at the lower-ground area. On high ground, we saw a variety of fruit trees (durian, mango, jackfruit, and other tropical fruits).

I don't know why, but somehow I felt at ease with this place. Maybe because I had been to Grandma's durian orchard many times years ago and grew up with the local landscape. The fruit orchard, the local variety of grasses and weeds, and the salty breeze in the air made me feel at home. (We were only a kilometer from the sea coast.) I guess this was the closest thing to returning home at the time.

Upon arrival, we went to see the village leader, Comrade Visna, pronounced "Wisna." The meeting with Comrade Visna was very courteous and friendly. This was a big contrast to when we met Ta-Heng. Comrade Visna gave us a brief introduction to the village. He said there were about a hundred families in this village, or around five hundred people. We had four work groups: men group, women group, senior group, and youth group. Each person would be assigned to each group based on their age and sex.

He then took us to a vacant house and said, "This will be your new home."

It was an elevated house, like any Cambodian rural farmhouse. It was about 1,200 square feet in a rectangular shape. This was considered plenty of square feet for ten people per local standard at the time. We were also pleasantly surprised by the good condition of the house. There were no holes in the roof, at least those we could not see. We only noticed a few holes in the walls. We now knew how to patch a wall with palm leaves, so we had no worries at all. The foundation and wood floor were in good condition. The place also was not too dusty.

We were given one week to get settled. Grandpa and Uncle Chin went out to greet and meet other families in the village. Uncle Hoang took us, the three boys, to catch some fish along the seashore. The three aunts cleared the weeds and shrubs around the property. Within a few days, we turned the house into our home.

A week quickly went by, and a new Monday arrived. We headed out to report for work. Similar to the Cement Factory, there was the senior group, men group, women group, and youth group. Unlike the Cement Factory, in this village not everyone got to work in the paddy fields all the time. Some weeks, the men group went to work in the paddy fields for four days a week. The men would take a day to go out to catch fish along the sea coast. Similarly, the women group might work in the paddy fields for three days and go to work in the fruit orchard for two days. Sometimes the group just went out to the local forest to pick wild fruits and mushrooms. The changes in work varieties and environments really helped to make the work less taxing, and people felt less stressed. These work activities were very similar to what we used to do many years ago whenever we visited Grandma's durian orchard. No wonder we really felt like we had returned home.

The food supply was much better. Rice quantity was adequately distributed. Also, fruits and fresh seafood were given out every week. You see, whenever a group went out to pick fruit or catch fish, whatever produce the village work group brought back that day would be distributed to all families in the village based on a family head count. Lives were really better. Everyone in this village was happy and nice to one another.

In this new village, there was no clear distinction between old comrades and newcomers. We really could not tell who the old comrades were. And who were the newcomers? Another thing I noticed was that almost every family here had a dog or a cat. In the Cement Factory, I never saw newcomers have a pet. I guess when people did not have enough to eat, pets would not be a priority. Soon we picked up a puppy too.

They said time flies when life is good. Soon another year went by. Now it was March 1977. One day we were all shocked to learn that Comrade Visna, our nice village leader, was taken away by Ongka. And a new leader, Comrade Sokun, pronounced "Sock Koon," was assigned to manage this village. And Comrade Sokun was not local. He had been sent from Kampong Chnam, a different province.

We, the villagers, were not told why Comrade Visna was taken away. There was a rumor that one of the men in the village saw Comrade Visna taken away with his hands tied behind his back. This appeared to be very serious. But nobody would dare to ask about him. Anyway, life in the village went on. There was no visible change under the new leadership of Comrade Sokun.

But about five weeks after Comrade Sokun's arrival, without any warning, Comrade Sokun called out names of ten families, and we were one of the ten. He added, "The ten families were chosen by Ongka to be relocated."

He told us to pack and get ready to be moved two days from now. But he did not tell us where we were going to. And we were given no opportunities to ask any questions. He simply said, "Get packed, and Ongka will send trucks to pick you up around dusk after tomorrow at this location."

As you can imagine, we all were very confused and worried and had many questions:

- What was the reason for this relocation?
- Why was my family selected? Was this a good or bad thing?
- Where would Ongka take us to? Was it very far from here?

- Why would the trucks come to pick us up at nighttime and not daytime?
- Was this really a relocation or one of the "taken to see Ongka" incidents?

Some two years later, after Vietnam kicked out the Khmer Rouge, we learned that the arrest of Comrade Visna, plus many of his peers in the surrounding villages, were a result of Khmer Rouge internal power struggle. A military commander of this region lost, and he escaped to Vietnam with several thousand of his men. And the winning Khmer Rouge faction came and arrested all the low-level leaders from this region, like Comrade Visna, who did not get a chance to escape to Vietnam. They were all executed, one by one, soon after they were rounded up.

Back to the village, we could not sleep much that last night because of the anxiety of not knowing where we would be taken to. What would happen to us? Sunlight finally broke out. We packed up, and by 4:00 p.m., we made our way to the designated waiting area along the road. When we got there, we saw two other families also waiting. We all looked confused and worried. Yet nobody would dare talk about the relocation.

By 6:30 p.m., two military trucks came by and stopped. Each family was assigned to a specific truck. One family at a time, we were told to get on the back of the Chinese-made military truck. The truck had no seats. We all needed to sit on the bare floor.

Our family got into the first truck. The driver closed the latch on the back door. He then pulled the truck cover down to close, as if he did not want us to see where we were heading to. By the time everyone got on the truck, it was already dark outside. The engine started, and we were on our way, heading toward Kampot.

I recalled the trucks made a couple of turns along the way. Because we had no visibility to the front view, plus it was dark outside, I could not tell what direction the truck was heading to nor where we were at any point during the ride.

I was curious whether the two trucks would go together or split up along the way. I kept peeking through the small gap on the truck's back door to see if I could still see the headlights of the second truck. Finally the two trucks slowed down and stopped along the roadside in the middle of nowhere.

The whole trip took about ninety minutes. We were told to get off the trucks here. There was no light from any house around. The only lights were the truck headlights. I could see rice paddy fields on both sides of the road, but I had no idea where we were.

One of the drivers pointed to the right and said, "There are two farmhouses over there. You all go to sleep for tonight. Our comrade will come to meet you here tomorrow."

We followed his directions and went to the abandoned farmhouses. The farmhouse had an elevated floor, but the stairs to go up were broken. It was late, so we simply found a clean spot with a roof cover to sleep for the night. We took comfort that we were all still alive and not sent to see Ongka (to be killed). But the anxiety still lingered in all of us. What would tomorrow be like? Where would we be going to?

The next day, we all woke up before sunrise. In fact, we could not sleep much at all last night. We kept thinking, *What would today be like? Who would come to meet us here? Where would they take us to from here?*

There was neither Starbucks nor a doughnut shop in sight. Fortunately most of us brought along cooked sweet potatoes or sweet corns, pots, and cups. We gathered some firewood to boil some water. We had sweet potatoes, sweet corns, and hot water for breakfast.

Around 9:00 a.m., we saw two Khmer Rouge men, each riding a bike, heading our way from a distance. Soon they arrived. They introduced themselves, Comrade Ta-Thom, pronounced "Ta Tom," and Comrade Samrin, pronounced "Sam reen." They told us they would be taking us to their village about fifteen kilometers from here.

Soon Ta-Thom and Samrin led the way. We followed and trekked through many paddy fields and finally reached the village around 3:00 p.m. Each family was taken to a pre-assigned vacant spot. We were asked to unpack and rest for the afternoon.

Around 5:00 p.m., Ta-Thom and Samrin came back to bring the new arrival family to have dinner at a big communal kitchen.

Ta-Thom explained, "In this village, nobody needs to cook at home. Each day we go to work with our designated work group. And each work group will come to the communal kitchen for lunch and dinner at a preassigned time slot."

Communal kitchen means that all harvest (rice, vegetables, meat, fish, poultry, and others) must go into the communal kitchen. Nobody in the village was allowed to cook meals at home. Any person or families found cooking meals at home would be facing severe retribution. Communal kitchen is the extreme form of government control. All food supply was 100 percent under Ongka control. This was one of the tools the Khmer Rouge used to manage people or suppress any possible uprising. I guess the Khmer Rouge was fully aware that organized rebellion would be difficult to start or sustain without food supply.

Our first meal at the communal kitchen was decent. We were given a small bowl of rice and one scoop of stir-fried vegetables with a few chunks of meat. (I know this meal is not a fine cuisine by any normal standard. But this was considered a good meal during the Khmer Rouge period.) After dinner, we went back to our house to sleep.

The next morning, Ta-Thom came to see us around 10:00 a.m. He brought the men from each family to gather wood and palm leaves to build a house. We were given three weeks to build our house. By week four, now about April 1977, Ta-Thom took each person to join the work group based on each person's age and sex. He added that during the weekday, men, women, and youth groups would stay and sleep at the group camp. Only the senior group would stay at home. Every morning, people would go to work together and lunch together at the communal kitchen. In the afternoon, the group also went to work until 4:00 p.m. and return to the communal kitchen for dinner after work. In the evening, every person must return to the designated camp to sleep. Everyone was only allowed to return home on Friday night for the weekend. And we needed to return to our work group camp by Sunday night.

After taking control of the country, the Khmer Rouge shut its door to the outside world. Communist China might be the only trading partner the Khmer Rouge had. The Khmer Rouge prioritized military hardware over farm equipment. This means during the Khmer Rouge period, 1975 to 1978, all heavy agriculture works had to be done by men, oxen, and cows. It was common to see farmers using cows and oxen to plow land and transport goods (pulling carts or hauling wagons). Many bulls are often castrated to become oxen. This made it easier for men to handle them. Oxen are usually yoked in pairs so they can move in unison. Similarly, cows are also yoked in pairs.

Back to the village. On the first day of work, Ta-Thom brought the men to their work group. Each man was assigned to handle two cows or two oxen. The cattle would be used to plow the field from 8:00 a.m. to noon. Ta-Thom also worked in the field alongside the men. Instead of using oxen and cows, Ta-Thom had two supercharged bulls, which were much larger in size than the other oxen and cows.

It is like when you go to a work site. You see many contractor men driving a Toyota Tacoma or Ford Ranger. And you see one man driving a supercharged V8, a Ford F250. This was as if he wanted to show who was in charge.

The men yoked the cows or oxen in pairs to plow the field in the morning. By noon, the men would hand over each pair of cows or oxen to a boy to graze in the afternoon. The boys needed to make sure the cattle were well-fed but not grazing on crops. The new arrival families had ten boys. Each boy was to be paired to two cows or two oxen.

The ten boys, including me, showed up at the field at noon. One by one, each boy was assigned to handle two cows or two oxen. Next up was boy number seven. He was assigned to take care of Ta-Thom's two big bulls. These two bulls were much larger in size than the other oxen and cows. These bulls had a huge intimidating head, two big horns, and an imposing neck muscle. The first bull was the bigger of the two. He had a dark brown head up to the neck and a white spot above his eyes. Ta-Thom named him White Eye. The second bull had yellow skin all the way up and a black tail. Ta-Thom called him Black Tail.

As boy number seven was approaching White Eye, the first bull charged at him, and the boy fell to the ground. Boy number seven moved on to the next pair of cows or oxen. Now Boy number eight was up, to be assigned to Ta-Thom's bulls. He just witnessed what happened to boy number seven. He approached the bulls nervously. White Eye also tried to charge boy number eight.

But this time Ta-Thom pulled the rope tight so the boy did not get pushed over. Up next was me, boy number nine. Although I had experienced and handled cattle in the last twelve months, I also saw what had just happened to boy number seven and eight. I moved forward nervously but calmly while looking straight at White Eye. The bull also looked at me. I saw his head still held high.

While everyone was holding their breath, I moved forward steadily. I saw him wagging his tail gently. This was a sign that the bull was still in relaxed mode. I moved another step closer and was able to pet him, just above his right eye. To everyone's surprise, White Eye did not attempt to charge me. Instead he calmly closed both his eyes and accepted me.

Now with more confidence, I made my move toward Black Tail, the second bull. Black Tail also closed both of his eyes as I extended my hand out to touch him and allowed me to pet him. I became the boy to take care of the big boss bulls. I learned later that for many months now, many boys and men were assigned to take care of Ta-Thom's two bulls. But nobody was able to stay because these two bulls did not accept anyone until I came along.

Isn't it amazing! I think humans and animals also have this instinct. You know you like a person or not very quickly. And as you read on, you will find how this faithful connection later changed my life.

My younger brother, boy number ten, was assigned to take care of the last two cows. Each morning we both would attend class until 11:00 a.m. Most of the lesson was learning about Ongka.

> Ongka led a revolution and chased away foreign oppressors, the capitalist Americans, and its puppet government in Phnom Penh. All Cambodians had been liberated. With Ongka's great leadership, we now have full control of our own destiny. Ongka loves us, the Youth League, more than our own parents. We must trust Ongka. We must be wholeheartedly loyal to Ongka. And we must report to Ongka if we see anyone do or say something bad against Ongka.

After the class, we would go to the communal kitchen for lunch. After lunch, my brother and I would go to the field to pick up our two cows and two bulls and herd them out to graze. All drafted cattle had their noses pierced and inserted with a rope. Normally a rope was about three meters long. The handler would hold on to one end of the rope, and the other end would be tied to the piercing on a cow or ox. This way he could manage and handle the cattle at will (left, right, go, and stop).

Normally we would herd the cattle to graze at either open-space areas with grass or the walkway between rice fields. In open-space areas, we could let the cattle roam free to graze on grass. One boy could handle four to six cattle while they were grazing. This was where a few boys could team up, one boy to look after all the group's cattle while the other boy could go to find food. At the end of the day, the boys would share the catch equally between them.

But sometimes grasses run out of open space because of overgrazing. Then I would need to herd my bulls to graze along the walkway between paddy fields. Each rice field is separated by levees about knee-high and about three feet wide. This would become the walkway between paddy fields. There were many miles of walkways between these paddy fields with plenty of grass. But it was more taxing to graze the cattle on these walkways because in addition to grasses on these walkways, there were also rice crops on both sides of these walkways, and the cattle loved to graze on rice crops. If grass were the main course for the cattle, rice crops would be dessert, and they loved rice crops. A person could only handle two cattle when grazing on these walkways.

Because the walkways were narrow and could only fit one cattle at a time, I would have one bull in front of me and the other one right behind me. My right hand would be holding a rope tied to the front bull. My left hand needed to hold a second rope tied to the second bull behind me. I needed to constantly watch the two bulls, the front one and back one, and prepare to pull the rope to make sure they didn't graze on the rice crop.

After handling the two bulls for a few weeks, I learned the bulls are also quite smart. When the bull was sensing you were not watching them tightly, they would extend their neck to reach for the crop. When this happened, I would need to pull in the bull immediately. White Eye was very well behaved, while the other one, Black Tail, would try to test my cattle-handling skills and patience every now and then.

So I put Black Tail right behind me. His head was literally next to me with the shorter rope; thus it was easier for me to control him. I put the well-behaved bull, White Eye, in front of me. His head was furthest away from me. Since it was more taxing to graze the cattle along these walkways between the paddy fields, people normally did not prefer to graze the cattle here. This means we had more grasses here, and the bulls only needed two hours to fill up, whereas in the open-field zone, the bulls needed four hours to graze.

Once the bulls were fed, I would bring the bulls to the river or lake to get a drink, normally at the end of the day. After the drink, I would clean the bulls. At the end of each day, my brother would return his two cows to the men handler, well-fed and cleaned. I returned my two big bulls well-fed and also cleaned to Ta-Thom's home. And I believed Ta-Thom and his wife noticed that I took good care of their bulls and they appreciated it.

By July 1977, food rations were getting less and less by the day. The communal kitchen did not have enough rice. They would mix rice and cassava or sweet corn. Each meal, we only had about half the portion we needed (half bowl of rice or cassava, one scoop of vegetable, and no meat or chicken). During spare time, people would go out to the lake, river, and paddy fields to catch something to eat.

When I returned the two bulls to Ta-Thom's home in the evening, Ta-Thom or his wife sometimes would hand me some food to eat. I guess they knew me and other newcomers were hungry. Sometimes they gave a bit more food and told me to share with my younger brother. You see, food shortages were only for the newcomers. For old comrades, they had a separate communal kitchen. Ideally communism means the state would distribute goods and services "equally" to everyone. But in practice, this process was polluted by political and personal bias.

My first exposure to marijuana was with Ta-Thom. When I returned White Eye and Black Tail in the late afternoon, sometimes Ta-Thom asked me to fetch a bucket of water for the bulls to drink. When I returned with a bucket of water, Ta-Thom would pour some ash from a big bamboo smoke pipe into the bucket of water. He would stir to mix the water and ash together.

He then said, "Now let the bulls drink the water."

This happened maybe once a week.

As a young boy, I was curious, so I asked him, "Why did you add the ash to the water? What does it do?"

He replied, "The ash was burnt marijuana. Added to water, the bulls drink it, and it makes the bulls stronger."

A few months had passed since I met Ta-Thom and took care of his two bulls. I remembered one day I found my right eye was red and irritated. I rubbed it a few times with my hand. Because there was no eye drops or any medical treatment, my eye condition was getting worse by the day. Each night when I slept, my right eye would have so much discharge that it was covered with sleep. Each morning I could barely open my right eye when I woke up. But I still needed to show up and take care of the bulls every day.

Fortunately Ta-Thom noticed something was wrong with my eye. He asked me. I told him my right eye was hurting. He looked at my eye. Without a second thought, he climbed up a coconut tree and cut down a half-dozen young coconuts. He cut a small opening on a young coconut and asked me to look up. He then gently poured the coconut juice into my sore eye. My eye felt cool, good, and relieved. I could feel my eye was getting better after the first treatment.

When I woke up the next morning, I noticed there was less discharge at night and less sleep covering my eye. I said thank you to him when I saw him the next day. He continued to give me the young coconut juice treatment at the end of each day for a week, and my eyes were cured.

After forty-plus years, I still vividly remembered the day the two bulls allowed me to pet their heads and accepted me. This faithful connection I had with these two bulls saved my eyesight, and it is no exaggeration for me to say it changed my life too. You see, during that time, only men in Ta-Thom's position would have the authority to pick coconut fruit. No other cow or oxen handlers would be able to do this. Luckily it appeared Ta-Thom knew young coconut juice could cure sore eyes. And if not for Ta-Thom's kindness, I could have gone blind.

I saw a lady who had a small cut on her leg, just below her knee. Because there was no antiseptic plaster to treat it during the Khmer Rouge period, the small cut became a chronic open wound, and years later the doctor needed to amputate her leg because the wound was infected and had damaged her leg bone. That lady was my aunt.

By September 1977, the food shortage had become much more severe. At the communal kitchen, each meal a person was given a bowl of congee, or rice porridge. The bowl is about the same size for Vietnamese Pho soup. But each bowl of congee would have no more than two spoons of rice and two to three spoons of chopped vegetables. The rest was simply filled with water, not chicken or beef broth. Every newcomer was starving and seriously malnourished. Yet we still had to perform hard labor work every day unless one was sick. People were so hungry that they would catch anything that moved (fish, crab, frog, and snake) and eat them.

For my younger brother and me, we teamed up so one person could herd two cows and two bulls while the other person could use the time to find food, like catching crabs, frogs, and fish and pick some wild fruit. If you recall, in the past when we went to the paddy fields to catch crabs and frogs, if something in the hole felt soft, we would move on to the next because what was inside the hole was likely to be a snake.

Now, as the food shortage was getting worse, I would be willing to take more risks to get some food. I would use the stick to spear into the hole repeatedly until I felt no struggle inside. This told me the snake might be dead or unconscious and I could now pull it out safely. I would pull the dead or unconscious snake out and cut off the head immediately to make sure it never woke up again. It turned out that snake tasted really good and was a good source of very lean white meat.

As the food shortage was becoming more severe, it was also becoming harder and harder to find fish, frogs, and crabs or any wild creatures to catch. Everyone would be willing to explore new sources of food. People would catch any creatures on land that could move to eat (grasshoppers, crickets, lizards, snails, rats, and so on).

I meant we cleaned up all crickets and bugs from the rice paddy fields without the need to use any pesticides. We figured out a way to hook and catch crested lizards to eat. We learned how to set up traps to catch squirrels and farm rats. We turned over every dead tree trunk and stone and caught any creatures hiding beneath it to eat. They all are good sources of protein.

At this phase of starvation, I saw people, myself included, would behave like any animal in the wild. All day you were thinking of how to get food to eat and how to steal food to eat and avoid being caught. If you were lucky to get more food than you could finish, you would try to hide it for your next meal versus giving it to others. I saw brothers fighting with one another for food, and I am not talking about kids.

On one Sunday afternoon while I was lying on my double-deck bed in the youth camp, I saw a large Tokay gecko about twelve inches long on the roof. Under normal situations, most people would be scared and try to chase it away. At the time, all I could think of was how to catch it to eat. I spent a few days observing its behavior and its commute route.

After two days of observation, I noticed this big gecko frequently moved between this roof and the tree at the back of the camp. I used palm leaves to make a small tunnel along its path. The palm leaves would act as camouflage. Like most wild animals, this gecko was very wary of its surroundings. On day one, the gecko paused when it saw the tunnel. It inspected, moved in very cautiously, and got through the tunnel. By day three, the gecko began to move naturally through my tunnel without any hesitation.

I knew it was now the right time to set up the trap. I used nylon string to make a round trap. I tied one end of the nylon string to a steady tree branch and carefully placed the trap precisely around the circumference of the tunnel. I then camouflaged the nylon string with more palm leaves. The round trap had a circumference big enough for the big gecko to put its head through without any obstruction.

When the big gecko extended its front leg to move forward, its claws would reach out, touch, and get caught up by the trap. The nylon trap would catch and tighten the big gecko by the neck. The gecko would struggle to get away. The trap would tighten up more as the gecko struggled and eventually choke it to death. The trap was set up on the evening of day four. I went to check my trap the morning of day five. The trap worked out as planned. My brother and I had a satisfying meal, and we were ready for our next hunt.

Sad to say, not all food hunting plans ended well. There was a mom whose three-year-old son was so hungry at night, the boy cried and asked his mother for food. The next day, the mom went to work. It so happened her group's work was to harvest sweet potatoes for the communal kitchen. While digging and collecting the sweet potatoes, she snuck out two small sweet potatoes and hid them in her pocket. Unfortunately Ongka saw her and sent a person to watch and follow her every move that day. That night, Ongka continued to watch her at home.

The mom made a small fire. She then buried the two sweet potatoes in the hot ash. When the boy asked for food late at night, in darkness, the mom quietly went out to pick up the potatoes to feed her boy. Ongka had been watching her and caught her in the act. On a Saturday all-village meeting,

Ongka paraded the mom and young child onto the stage with both of their hands tied behind their back.

As they stood on the stage, the young mom looked down worriedly, and the poor young boy hugged her leg nervously. He clearly was scared but did not know what was going on. Ta-Thom denounced her for pilfering communal food supply as selfish and counterrevolution. Other Khmer Rouge leaders joined in to condemn her larceny.

One Khmer Rouge leader went much further to say that such looting of communal food had caused serious food shortages for all villagers. Therefore, Ongka could not allow this to continue. (This was the most extreme example of fact distortion I had ever heard.)

But the message he delivered was very clear: If any one of you, the newcomers, try to loot communal food, let this be the lesson. We are watching you, and Ongka would punish you. The young mother admitted what she did was wrong. She pleaded to Ta-Thom and other Khmer Rouge leaders for forgiveness. After about thirty minutes of public humiliation, they took the mom and the young boy away to see Ongka, and we never saw them again. (He likely killed them.)

Food shortages and starvation for newcomers went on for many more months. We were so malnourished that people literally had no flesh, with bare skin wrapping around their skeletons. Starving people became weak, and soon weak people became sick people. Very soon we had the very young and very old people dying every day. My poor grandpa passed away under that horrific condition. With great sadness, none of us was able to see Grandpa on his last day. Only Grandma was at home at the time. We all were out in our work group camp and were not aware or allowed to take leave to return home.

My grandpa was very honest, a brilliant accountant, and, more importantly, a very decent man. He loved his family. He worked very hard to support his family, a wife, ten children, and seven grandchildren. His spotless integrity and unparalleled reputation opened doors for him to become a senior executive in Air Cambodia.

Three months before the Khmer Rouge victory in 1975, his boss saw the Khmer Rouge, the communists, was coming. The big boss, the owner of Air Cambodia, was planning to move his whole family to France within a month. (Why France? Cambodia was a French colony until 1953. This heritage enabled many people in Cambodia and France to have cultural exchange and business association.)

The big boss offered Grandpa and his family (ten of us) to go to France with them on the same plane. Grandpa gratefully declined the offer because Grandpa loved Cambodia. He could never—in fact, nor did most Cambodians—anticipate how a beautiful country like Cambodia could turn into a killing field. I love you, Grandpa, and rest in peace.

Life moved on in the village. Despite the severe starvation and the tragic human suffering, Ongka had a new assignment for us, the malnourished newcomers. Ongka sent the work groups to cut down trees in the nearby forest to make land for a new plantation. Ongka's propaganda slogan at the time was "More new land. More food." Several hundred men and women were sent to clear the forest. All the work, the chopping down of trees and cutting the downed tree into short logs so people could haul it away, were done manually. Not a single power tool was used.

This was a pristine and thick tropical forest that had been there for hundreds of years, maybe thousands. The forest was divided into several sections: A, B, and C. Each section was about twenty acres. The men and women work groups would spend two weeks to clear all the trees and vegetation from one section of the forest. By week three, the workers would move on to cut down trees in a new section of the forest, called section B, while section A would be left to dry out in the sun. By week four, the leaves in section A turned yellow and dried up. We started a fire to burn section A, while the men and women continued to cut down more sections of the forest.

When we burned section A, we started the fire from the outside. The goal was to trap and burn the wild animals so we could eat them. The burning took about a week for the ashes to cool down. After it was cooled down, everyone moved in to hunt for food during break time. In most cases, we found charred squirrels, wild rats, snakes, and occasional hogs and deer.

It was a very risky business to hunt for food on the charred forest floor. This was because most of us, the newcomers, walked in bare feet, as we did not have any shoes or sandals during the Khmer Rouge period. If you were not careful, your feet could either get burned or cut while scouting the charred forest floor for food. And a simple cut or burn could be fatal when we had no antibiotics and antiseptic to treat the cut or burned foot.

You see, when you were hunting on a newly burned forest floor in bare feet, because we had no shoes or sandals, the ash on the surface might be cool, but there were still some tree trunks burning below the ground. You might see no smoke or feel no heat on the surface. But deep down, the tree trunk was still burning. If you stepped on it, you would step into a fire pit below, and your foot could get burned badly.

I saw several people got hurt pretty badly, unfortunately. So you really needed to use a stick and check before you step on any ground. Also, people cut smaller tree trunks at an angle and ground level. After the burning, you might not see the sharp tree trunk because the ashes covered it. This buried small tree trunk cut at an angle would act as a sharp blade buried under the ash. When you stepped on it with a bare foot, the sharp tree trunk would cut your foot. Again, this otherwise simple cut could become a serious infection and may even be fatal when you don't have any medical treatment.

Back to the charred forest. After the burning, this virgin land would need to be plowed. All the root buried beneath, some were big and went deep, needed to be dug up and cut into short pieces by hand so it could be moved by men to the side without any power tools before we could plant sweet corn.

One day while we, other kids and me, were herding our cattle to graze in the open space near the charred forest, we saw a group of about twenty prisoners was escorted to work on the charred forest. Each prisoner had his right hand tied to the other prisoner's right hand in front and behind. Each prisoner's left hand was also chained to one another in the same fashion. All the prison guards were in their teens, fifteen to eighteen years old.

All the prisoners were hungry, skinny, and severely malnourished. A majority of the prisoners were men and a couple of women. It was my first time ever to see prisoners during the Khmer Rouge period. This was because the Khmer Rouge was known to have a "no prisoner policy." The

Khmer Rouge was well-known to prefer to kill the offender instead of holding them as prisoners so as to not waste valuable resources, food. As a young boy, I was wondering, *What crime did these people commit?*

These prisoners were paraded past us with both hands chained to one another. While some of us were eating some charred animals we found on the burned forest floor, I happened to eat a piece of rat leg, and I threw away a piece of leg bone. A few prisoners saw it and rushed out to fight for it.

One prisoner got to it first, quickly picked it up from the ground, put it into his mouth, and chewed the bone to eat. A few kids saw and felt sorry for these starving prisoners. The kids threw out bits and pieces of charred meat and bone. These starving prisoners rushed to pick up whatever they could reach and eat it.

A young Khmer Rouge guard saw the prisoners run out of line. He yelled "No!" He quickly ran over and whipped the prisoners one by one.

Despite the harsh punishment, these poor prisoners were so hungry and desperate that they would still take the risk to pick up any food scraps they could find. It was the most horrific scene of human cruelty toward another human I ever saw and could never forget.

It was now December 1977, and the rice crop was ready to be harvested. The village celebrated another successful harvest. New crops had filled the village food storage. The meal portion at the communal kitchen had improved greatly. With adequate meals and nutrition for a couple of months, we were able to regain some physical strength. Mysteriously the village food supply was disappearing from the store very quickly again. There was a strong suspicion that Ongka had taken the food to trade with communist China for more guns and ammunition. By May 1978, we had entered a new cycle of food shortage. And the food supply situation was again getting worse by the day.

Vietnam Invasion

It was now about November 1978. We had completed two rice planting and harvesting seasons in the new village. I guess more correctly, I should say we had survived two annual cycles of starvation in the new village.

Around December 1978, during a Saturday all-village meeting, Ta-Thom suddenly condemned Vietnam as an evil country. He went on to tell tales of century-old animosity between Vietnam and Cambodia. We all knew Viet Cong and the Khmer Rouge not only won the war in 1975, but they both had been allies of communist China. Therefore, we were quite surprised to hear this denunciation from the Khmer Rouge.

Within a few weeks, the villagers were told Vietnam had invaded Cambodia. At the time, we had no access to any news. We did not have much information about the Vietnam invasion. Why did Vietnam invade Cambodia? How far had the Vietnamese force entered Cambodia? Which part of the border did the Vietnamese come in? You see, Cambodia and Vietnam have about 1,113 kilometers of a shared border. And the Khmer Rouge did not give us any information about a Vietnam invasion, except what the Khmer Rouge propaganda machine told us, "Vietnam soldiers had killed many Cambodian civilians, women and children, whenever they moved in and captured a village. So for everyone's safety, we must pack and move west."

We assumed the reason we were told to get packing and to head west was because the Vietnamese forces had already entered Cambodia. Many newcomers were not only happy, privately, to hear about the Vietnam invasion, we were also secretly praying and hoping that the Vietnamese would get here as quickly as possible so we would be rescued from this hell and suffering.

For the time being, we still needed to pack up per Ongka's instruction and be ready to move. Ta-Thom asked all the men to load up the oxen and cow carts with food supplies. Some men without an oxen cart would need to carry sacks of rice, about twenty-five pounds, on their shoulder. The whole village began to move west together the next day. We trekked across paddy fields and walked past many villages. Each day we walked for three to four hours and rested by noon. This would give us time to find a place to rest, find water, cook, and resupply our food.

The villagers would find a place to rest together across an open space and sleep under a tree if you could get the spot first, like a group campsite, except we did not have any tents. Some nights, we would find a dry spot and rest in a paddy field under the sky. Fortunately it was a dry season, else we might have to deal with the rain while we were on the move as we had no plastic tarp sheets or raincoats at all.

For the first weeks, Ta-Thom and all his villagers were trekking together, heading west. Ironically, we did not have any food shortage when we were escaping from the Vietnam invasion. This is because Ta-Thom and other Khmer Rouge did not put much restrictions on our activities when we were on the run. I guessed these Khmer Rouge leaders had to be alerted and looked out for their own safety first because they did not want to be captured by the Vietnamese. Plus, it was not easy to manage and control a big group of people while on the move. So we, the villagers, got some breaks and were able to find our own food (rice, chicken, fish, and fruit). Sometimes we even found a pig to kill and would share the meat whenever we got to an abandoned village. We never had this much food and good meat to eat for a long time, specifically two years.

Each family finally was able to cook whatever they could find, no more communal kitchen. To me, as a young child, this was my first realization of what humans can do with freedom. Freedom drives motivation, creativity, and independence.

Along the way, we encountered other villagers who were also escaping and moving westward with Ongka. As more and more people from different villages mingled and moved together, it was clear Ta-Thom and other Khmer Rouge leaders were no longer in control of their villagers. We, the newcomers, began to look for opportunities not to continue westward with Ongka. But we also needed to be very vigilant. We could not afford to try something silly and get caught. Remember, with Ongka we only had one strike. If anyone or family get caught staying behind waiting to defect to the

Vietnamese, you and your whole family would be considered a traitor(s), and the Khmer Rouge would kill the whole family without hesitation.

We had been travelling west with Ta-Thom and other villagers for about two weeks now. The group entered a mountain and trekked into the forest. We still had food supplies to last at least ten days. But we had run out of salt. We started to cook food without salt.

After eating food without salt for two days, we started to have no appetite for food, and by day four, we no longer wanted to eat anything without salt. One day, we were trekking in the forest. By noon, each family found a spot to rest under the trees across the forest floor. We saw about twenty young Khmer Rouge soldiers running toward us and heading west.

These soldiers quickly called out without pausing, "You must go now! Vietnamese are coming!" And they continued to run westward nervously.

I recalled a similar scene four years ago when the Lon-Noh soldiers were escaping for their lives before the Khmer Rouge entered Phnom Penh. This time we saw Ta-Thom and other Khmer Rouge leaders hurriedly pack up, flee westward, and abandon us in the process. I guess they figured they had no time to round up the villagers to come along.

We recognized this meant the Vietnamese would not be far away and this was the opportunity for us to make a move. We, about twenty families, decided to stay put in the forest, as no more Khmer Rouge was around to bother us. The afternoon went by without any incident. A few men went out to check what resources were available nearby in this forest. A man found a lake about a half-kilometer away.

We all moved closer to the lake. Each family found a place to rest in the woods along the east shore. The lake had an oval-like shape, about one kilometer in length and maybe five hundred meters in width. Soon it was sunset, and the twenty families spent a quiet night in the woods along the east shore of the lake.

The next morning, the air was fresh. The place was calm and very peaceful. After breakfast, about 9:00 a.m., Uncle Chin and I walked to the lakeshore. Suddenly we heard several gunshots at a distance and people speaking at a distance. But the volume was too low to tell if it were Cambodian or Vietnamese. We scanned across the opposite shore to see if we could spot any people, but we could not find anyone.

Uncle Chin turned to me. "Let's move over there and hide first. We don't know if they are Khmer Rouge or Vietnamese."

We moved to hide in the brush and kept scanning the shore for signs of people. The voices were getting louder as time went on. A few minutes later, it was clear the voices were in Vietnamese. But we still could not spot any people. We continued to hide in the brush and kept scanning across the shore.

Some ten minutes later, we finally saw five to six Vietnamese soldiers in the Viet Cong signature hard hat coming out of the forest and walking toward the lake. Uncle Chin took off his white T-shirt and tied it to a stick to make a white flag. Uncle Chin put up his white flag (a universal symbol of surrender), and we both walked out of the brush slowly with both hands high in the air.

The Vietnamese soldiers spotted us. They were approaching us cautiously. One soldier had his AK-47 pointing at Uncle Chin and me while the other soldiers were scanning to see if any Khmer Rouge were around. We both stood still with both hands up, waiting for them to come closer. I could see more and more Vietnamese soldiers coming out of the woods and walking to the lakeshore.

We called out to inform the other people, "Vietnamese soldiers are here. Do not move, and please put your hands up."

As the Vietnamese soldiers came closer, they asked, "Any Pol Pot around?"

Initially we did not know what they meant by "Pol Pot." You see, in the past four years under the Khmer Rouge, we were not only completely shut off from the outside world, but we also had no idea who the Khmer Rouge leader was. We finally figured out the Vietnamese called the Khmer Rouge "Pol Pot" because Pol Pot was the name of the Khmer Rouge supreme leader.

Some of us spoke Vietnamese. We told them the Khmer Rouge had moved that way last night. We asked the Vietnamese how to get to Kampot. The Vietnamese pointed to a trail where they were coming out of earlier. They told us to strictly follow the trail up the hill and go down again to follow the trail. They said this would lead us to National Highway 3. They told us they had scanned and cleared the trail for land mines. And they warned us not to go off the trail to get water or pick wild fruit to eat, as the Khmer Rouge might have laid mines. They said there would be a Vietnamese base camp down the hill, about twenty kilometers from here. We could get food and other supplies there.

With mixed emotion, we said thank you and goodbye to the Vietnamese soldiers. It was very strange to welcome a foreign force and truly appreciate them to come and rescue us. At the same time, we knew they were invading our country.

We trekked through the forest, strictly staying on the trail, winding up the hill.

The trail was only about two meters wide, not big enough for any four-wheel vehicles to come through. Soon we got to the top and descended the other side to complete the twenty-kilometer journey. We got to the Vietnamese base camp at about 4:00 p.m. This base camp was like a temporary military supply and communication center. There were a half-dozen big tents and maybe ten smaller tents. About two hundred soldiers were stationed there. From their accent, we could tell they were North Vietnamese, plus a few Cambodians. We learned the Cambodians were former Khmer Rouge who had escaped to Vietnam in late 1977, and now they returned to fight off their former buddy, the Khmer Rouge.

We all went to get some food and much-needed salt. With the presence of many more Vietnamese soldiers at the base camp, we finally felt like we could see the light after spending months in a dark tunnel, so safe and secure at last. We all found a spot to rest and cook dinner. We, the twenty families, together celebrated our first night of freedom by toasting one another. The dinner was a simple meal of rice, some chicken, and vegetables, and the food tasted so much better with salt. We went to bed and rested soon after dark, as we knew we still had a long walk tomorrow.

The next morning, most of us woke up before sunrise. I guess since most of us had not been to our home city for four or five years, we were looking forward to heading back. After breakfast, we asked the Vietnamese soldiers for directions to Kampot and other cities. First we all needed to walk another fifty kilometers on a dirt road to get to National Highway 3. This would be a two- to three-day journey.

So we went to the Vietnamese base camp to ask for a few days of food supplies. We hit the road by 9:00 a.m. We walked at least four hours per day, stopped to rest at noon, and found a place to rest along the roadside each night. We basically walked through a big, abandoned rubber plantation, which must have been abandoned for many years. The plantation ground was covered by overgrown weeds and brushes.

If you don't know what a rubber tree looks like, you would think it is a forest full of trees and brush. And the long dirt road probably was built, linking the plantation to National Highway 3, so trucks could come in to haul raw rubber to the processing plant.

We finally arrived at National Highway 3 at noon on day three. It was a big milestone, another step closer to our home city. We knew if we continued to head south along National Highway 3, we would get to Kampot. But we still did not know how far away we were from Kampot.

At this junction, the twenty families started to split up, each heading to their home destination. We said goodbye and best wishes to one another. We walked for about an hour and saw a sign that said seventy kilometers to Kampot. We decided to find a place to rest for the night on the roadside.

During that time, the road literally had no vehicle traffic, except for the occasional military truck. The next day, we continued walking along National Highway 3 to Kampot. Along the way, we also saw other families recently liberated from the Khmer Rouge, and like us, they were trying to get back to their respective home city.

Whenever we found a place to rest at noon or night, we would talk to different families and share and exchange stories or our experiences during the Khmer Rouge regime over the last four years.

Listening to these people, we learned one common theme, that all newcomers were treated as second-class citizens and every aspect of the newcomer's life, work, food, and other provisions were allocated based on this classification. We also heard many tragic stories. Almost all the families had lost loved ones either by starvation or illness during the Khmer Rouge regime. In the most tragic one, we met two sisters, twenty-two and twenty-four years old, who used to have six people in their family (Mom, Dad, two older brothers, and them). In mid-1977, for unexplained reasons, Ongka took away all newcomer men from the village and killed them all. Her dad and two older brothers were taken away at midnight, and they never heard or saw them again. Their mom was traumatized, understandably. She became very sick, and when starvation hit the village six months ago, she could no longer hold on. She died.

Listening to all these sad and tragic stories of other families, we realized how fortunate we had been. Despite all the hardship we went through, at least we had only lost Grandpa. Nine of us somehow survived the ordeal. We made it not because we were stronger or better than other families. I think we were lucky. Maybe someone high above looked after us. Take me as an example. If it were not for the faithful connection I had with Ta-Thom's two bulls, my eyes could have gone blind, and I might not have survived.

It took us another four days to finally see a sign, "Welcome to Kampot." We were very emotional to see the sign. It was like seeing your loved one again after many years. If we had cameras, I was pretty sure we would have taken a family photo with the sign and date stamped on it.

We entered the city very anxiously. We would turn right and left, looking at the houses on both sides of the street. Before the Khmer Rouge victory in 1975, many of the buildings and houses in Kampot were two or three stories high. Most of the ground floor was for commercial use (grocery stores, restaurants, tailor shops, hair salons, shoe shops, etc.). The second and third floors were mostly residential.

We were glad to see many buildings were still standing and in relatively good shape with no visible damage, and all needed a good wash down and a new coat of paint. But we noticed and were sad to see most of the doors and windows were damaged, and some had totally disappeared. When we arrived in January 1979, for the most part, Kampot was still a deserted city. This was two weeks after the Vietnamese took control of Phnom Penh and kicked out the Khmer Rouge.

We saw a majority of the buildings were still vacant. Only a few were occupied. This meant we were the early group of survivors who had arrived in Kampot after the Vietnam invasion. We continued to walk past the city center and crossed the main bridge. We were planning to turn right after crossing the bridge to head to Grandma's house.

But there was a barricade. A Vietnamese soldier guarding the post came out. "This area is off-limits to the public." (Remember, I mentioned earlier that Grandma's house was on a prime location in Kampot, right along the main river. The occupying Vietnamese certainly recognized this prime spot.)

Well, since we could not go to Grandma's place, we decided to go to her sister's house, which was just straight ahead as you came off the bridge, and it was just one block from the bridge. This was a main thoroughfare linking South Kampot to Kampot city center. We got to the house, and it was still vacant. We decided to settle in there.

After the Vietnam invasion, many Cambodians returned to their home city. Since all the property ownership documents had been destroyed or lost, there was no way for anyone to prove this property was mine or yours. After all, many owners probably did not survive the Khmer Rouge period. So all the buildings and land were open to be taken. The unwritten rules were "first come, first serve."

Grandma's sister's house was a two-story building. Like many buildings in Kampot, the doors and windows were damaged. Once we moved in, we realized why many doors and windows were destroyed. In our block, there were about twenty houses. All were two-story brick houses and built around the same time in the 1960s. Many kitchens had portable gas stoves and woodburning stoves.

When we entered each building to look for useful items, we often found bits and pieces of chairs, tables, or doors had been split up and turned into firewood. We also found remnants of table legs or doors that had been burned halfway and still rested on the stove opening. This suggested that during the Khmer Rouge period, some Khmer Rouge lived or were stationed in Kampot.

You see, many Khmer Rouge were rural peasants. They were so used to and only knew how to burn wood for cooking and lighting. They probably never saw or had any knowledge of the alternative, using gas for cooking. So when they were living in the city, there were no trees for them to cut down for firewood. If they needed firewood, the closest thing to wood were tables, chairs, doors, and windows.

I need to add, these were not the cheap, made-in-China furniture you get from big-box stores. Much of the dismantled furniture was once handcrafted fine furniture made of solid redwood. We were speechless to see such senseless destruction of properties in Kampot by the Khmer Rouge. Unfortunately this kind of ruination was not unique to Kampot. The same scene played out in many other cities across Cambodia in 1979.

In early 1979, Kampot literally had no government. The only official in charge of Kampot was the Vietnamese commander stationed at the block of nice houses near Grandma's house. And there was no public service of any kind in Kampot. All the water systems, power grids, and sanitation systems were either abandoned, damaged, or not working.

Back to the house, we cleaned up the house and made it our new home in Kampot. We found a water well across the street from the house, which became our source of water for everyday use. A few days later, one of Grandma's nieces showed up. Like us, she had recently escaped from the Khmer Rouge and just returned to her home city. The house we just cleaned up and occupied was her mother's house. She was in her forties.

Grandma and all of us were so happy to see her. We told her we would move next door and let her back in her house. We ended up living next to each other. We later found out, unfortunately, her mother (Grandma's sister), her husband, and one of her kids had passed away during the Khmer Rouge period. Now she was a widow with her ten-year-old son.

Each day Uncle Chin and Uncle Hoang would go out into the city center to scout vacant buildings looking for anything useful (food, pots, pans, tables, clothes, etc.) and valuables (jewelry and cash). Four years ago, when the Khmer Rouge evacuated the city, many people left behind all their belongings in the city. And these houses in the city had been abandoned, some even left untouched. Since we were the first few families who got to Kampot first, we were able to pick up useful items from these vacant houses.

For younger kids like us, my younger brother, Uncle Khieng, and I normally headed out to fish in the nearby river, and some days we fished along the seashore. These were the same areas we went fishing many years ago. We were very familiar with the neighborhood. We noticed there were many more fish now and the fish were bigger too. This was because in the last four years, during the Khmer Rouge period, not many people were around to fish in the surrounding areas. Therefore, the fish population and size had grown significantly. For the first four weeks, we spent each day searching for usable items and food gathering. We stored our food on the second floor. This way it was not too visible and harder for people to steal.

On days we did not go fishing, I sometimes would walk around in Kampot to check out each neighborhood. One day I saw a group of five to six young men had encircled a man at the wall of a building on the other side of the street. I was curious to find out what was going on. I crossed the street, and as I got closer, I saw one of the young men had kicked and called him "you evil bastard!" Another man spat at him. A third man pushed him down to the ground. A fourth man kicked him in the face, and the man's nose was bleeding.

A passerby saw the scuffle. He thought this was a petty fight among teenagers who had too much testosterone. He ran over and tried to stop the assault.

"What is going on? The Vietnamese soldiers may come soon. Let's not fight among ourselves, Cambodians."

One of the men said, "This motherfucker is a Khmer Rouge. He killed my older brother."

A second man pointed out, "This son of a bitch was heartless. He destroyed many families, and we should make him pay back."

A third man jumped up and kicked the guy in his face. His nose was bleeding profusely. Within a few minutes, a couple of Vietnamese soldiers with AK-47s ran over and broke up the assault. After the Vietnamese learned the man was a Khmer Rouge, they took him away.

If the Vietnamese soldiers did not come, I had no doubt the men would not stop the assault and the Khmer Rouge man would be seriously injured, if not killed right there. I could see the emotion of these men were very high. The memory of lost family members was still fresh, and I could not blame them. I had witnessed a few similar incidents at Kampot in early 1979. And this made me wonder. What if the Khmer Rouge man being kicked at was Ta-Thom? (Just a recap, Ta-Thom was the Khmer Rouge village leader, the owner of the two bulls I was assigned to take care of. He gave me food and young coconut juice to treat my eye sore and probably saved my eyesight.) What would I do if this man were him? Thank God I was spared from this dilemma.

A few days later, Grandma and I were walking in Kampot. Other people were walking up and down the street. We saw a mentally ill lady talking to herself and heading in our direction. This was the first time I had seen a mentally ill person on the street since we had arrived in Kampot four weeks ago.

As this lady got closer to us, Grandma and I moved right to make room for her to sneak past. Suddenly this lady turned back and called out Grandma's name, "Mrs. Kim So."

Grandma turned. "Did you call my name? Do we know each other? What is your name, Ma'am?"

The lady said, "You are Mrs. Kim So? And you have a son named Chin, correct?"

Grandma replied, "Yes, how do you know my son? Who are you?"

"I am Mrs. Wong. We used to live in the same village near the cement factory. My husband and your son Chin used to hang out together. Do you remember?"

We could not believe it. The mentally ill lady, at least we thought she was a few minutes ago, was now talking to us like a normal person, and she was someone we knew.

If you recall earlier, when we stayed in a village near the cement factory, Mr. Wong had hung himself because he could not find food to support his family. Even though he still had a stack of US dollars, it was worthless during the Khmer Rouge period.

Grandma replied, "Yes, we used to live in a village near the cement factory. Yes, I remember Mr. Wong. Are you and your family now living in Kampot too?"

The lady broke down and cried, "Oh, Mrs. Kim So. I no longer have a family. You know what happened to my husband. He hung himself years ago, and my kids, they are all gone too, died due to starvation and illness after your family moved out."

Grandma tried to comfort her and asked her to come to our place. Without warning, as if someone turned a switch on her back, the lady switched off and went away on her own and talked to herself again. Grandma explained to me that the poor lady had been traumatized by the death of her husband and children. We felt so sad for her, but we could not stop her.

As the day passed, we saw more and more people come and settle in Kampot. By March 1979, six weeks after we arrived, most of the buildings in Kampot now had been occupied. Our only water well supply was not able to catch up with demand due to the increased population. Yet there was no running water system.

The people in the neighborhood got together to discuss and develop rules for water usage. Everyone agreed that the water from the well was limited and this water should be reserved for drinking only. For washing and other usage, people must go and get the water from the river. It was about two blocks away, and the supply was more plentiful. I guess this was the early phase of self-government. Grandma's niece turned out to be quite active in the community, and she later become the official leader of this neighborhood group.

Life in Kampot seemed to settle down, at least for us as we got a decent stockpile of food, relatively speaking. But the city was still facing many challenges. First, the country still had no currency system. There were no public services of any kind, no hospital, no running water, no working electric power grid, and no sewage system to support an increasing city population.

Two months quickly went by. Uncle Chin decided to join a few men to go to Ha Tien, a border city in Vietnam. The main purpose of the trip was to buy some fishing gear and household items. These items would enable us to catch more fish and improve our lives.

Ha Tien was about fifty kilometers from Kampot. The group needed to make the journey by foot, as there was no public or private transportation of any kind in early 1979. One day, about a week after Uncle Chin's departure, my brother and I returned home from fishing. We saw Uncle Chin had returned from his Ha Tien expedition. We saw some new items laid on the floor (clothing, towels, etc.). I assumed he had bought them from Ha Tien.

Like any regular day, we were planning to clean the fish we had just caught so Grandma could cook them. But Uncle Chin told us, "Leave the fish aside for now. You can do it later. Go upstairs to see someone."

You see, during that period of time, we frequently saw new people arriving in Kampot as they had just been rescued or escaped from the Khmer Rouge. Many were extended family members, former neighbors, or friends. My brother and I obliged. We cleaned up and walked up a dark staircase, as we had no power and no lighting in the house. I was very curious to find out who this new person or visitor was.

Once we got upstairs, the second floor was dimly lit by daylight through a window. I could see Grandma, Aunt Lim, Aunt Leng, and a new lady. They sat in a circle and were chatting merrily. I could tell with certainty that I had seen or met this new lady in the past, but I simply could not recall her name or what her relationship was to the family.

I was not sure how much my brother knew about the new lady either. Anyway, we both stood there and just looked at them, the four women, as if we were waiting for an introduction. Grandma spotted us, my brother and I, standing by the stair. Grandma waved at us, signaling us to come closer.

"Come, look who is here. Come and see your mom."

When I heard "come and see your mom," I froze in disbelief for a few seconds and stood still in silence. Frankly, I longed to hear this, "Come and see your mom," countless times when I was younger and in my dreams for the last nine years, but it never came. So I was not sure this time was real. I turned and grabbed hold of my brother's hand, as if I were trying to confirm I was not in my dream.

As I grabbed his hand, my brother turned and looked at me, as if he asked me, "What should we do?" We both did not know what to do, how to respond at that moment.

Aunt Lim urged, "Quick, come and see your mother!"

We anxiously walked up to her and called, "Mom." She jumped up and hugged both of us tight and cried. You see, we had not seen or had any news about our parents for nine years, since I was five and my brother was four. In fact, I never had any expectations. Maybe I gave up hope that I would be able to see my parents again. Honestly, if it were not for Grandma and Uncle Chin, who still recognized Mom, I believe my brother and I would not be able to recognize her if we crossed paths with her on a street. And I don't believe she would be able to recognize us either.

I need to say this family reunion was nothing short of a miracle and I am truly blessed. During that period of time, many children in Cambodia became orphans. Because of similar scenarios, maybe the father was out of town when the Khmer Rouge evacuated the cities, and the families were split up. The father went to a village alone during the Khmer Rouge reign, whereas the mother and the kids ended up in a separate village. And during the Khmer Rouge period, the mother died.

Now after the Vietnam invasion, the kid and the father survived the ordeal, but they would not be able to recognize one another even if they saw each other on the street because the kid was too young when they split up from their father years ago.

Mom told us, after they left my brother and me at Grandma's house in 1970 during the civil war, they went to live in hiding in a small town near the Vietnam border to avoid possible political prosecution. She explained they left us with Grandma for our safety because they could be arrested at any time by the Lon-Noh government. And when the Khmer Rouge evacuated the people from cities across Cambodia in April 1975, Mom and Dad escaped to Vietnam because their instinct told them something was not right.

Mom added, after they got to Vietnam in 1975, they were looking for us (Grandpa, Grandma, and family) at the border town and hoped we also escaped to Vietnam. But after four weeks of searching and still no sign of us, they went to live in Ho Chi Minh City.

Mom and Dad heard the Khmer Rouge had been overthrown by Vietnam about eight weeks ago. Since then, they had also heard some Cambodians began to enter Vietnam to buy stuff. So two weeks ago, they decided to come to Ha Tien again, to look for us or at least hope to get some news about us.

You see, during the past nine years, Cambodia had gone through a civil war and genocide. We, the family and my parents, had been separated. We had absolutely no contact with each other, no mail, and no phone. And there was no newspaper or anyone we could ask to look for missing relatives. Despite all that, somehow Uncle Chin and my mom miraculously met in a marketplace. They both happened to be at the same place at the same time. And this encounter led to our family reunion. I can say this with certainty, the odds for Uncle Chin and my mom to meet at that marketplace in Ha Tien is no better than a person gettting hit by lightning.

Six

The Family on the Move Again

This happy family reunion had completely tossed out the family's original plan to settle in Kampot. We decided to move to Vietnam with Mom without any second thought. I guess there was nothing much we needed to consider. We simply assumed Vietnam would be better than Cambodia. After all, we had just survived the Khmer Rouge genocide. What else could be worse? We had nothing to lose.

Two days later, we packed up, and the family started walking at 8:00 a.m. to a town that bordered Vietnam, Ha Tien. We got to the border town around 4:00 p.m. and went to see the road leading to a bridge to get to Vietnam.

We only saw people walking from Vietnam to Cambodia, and nobody walked in the opposite direction or entered Vietnam. None of the Cambodians had passports to enter Vietnam officially in 1979, as the new Cambodian government had not fully formed yet.

Uncle Chin explained, although Cambodians could not enter Vietnam officially yet because there were no passports, there was a nonofficial channel for Cambodians to enter Ha Tien by boat. Uncle Chin led us to the shore on the bay not too far from the border town. From the shore, we could see Ha Tien across the bay.

Since this was an illegal channel, we all needed to hide and wait in the tall brush along the bay until dark. Soon it got dark, and about 8:00 p.m., Uncle Chin told us to look for a spotlight flashing three times from a boat out in the bay. Sure enough, we soon spotted three flashes in the bay.

Uncle Chin turned on his flashlight and returned the signal three times. The boat at a distance signaled back to acknowledge "message received." All we had to do now was wait for the boat to come closer to the beach. About twenty minutes later, in darkness, we saw a small fishing boat approaching. All ten of us were so excited to get onto the small boat, one person at a time so not to rock the boat too much.

The boat was probably twenty feet long and maybe three feet wide. As you can see, the boat was not much bigger than a canoe. The boat had six rows of seats, and each seat could barely fit two skinny persons. Luckily, we all were skinny and petite at the time. I am pretty sure, if we went onto the boat at my current body weight, it would sink for sure. The boat was powered by a small propeller engine, probably no bigger than a lawn mower engine.

Once we all sat down, the boat was barely a foot above the water. The boat started heading out into the bay and to Vietnam. I reached out and touched the water with my hand as the boat moved forward. The boat moved across the bay in darkness. No light was turned on to evade attention, I guess. And we saw thousands of bright and shiny sardines and anchovies lit by moonlight, swimming and jumping alongside the boat on the surface of the water. It was quite an amazing and beautiful scene, better than anything you can see in a man-made aquarium.

As we got closer to the Vietnam shore, the captain turned off the engine, again to evade attention. He paddled the boat to shore by hand. As the boat got closer to the shore and the water was about knee-deep, we got off the boat by stepping down into the water and walked to the shore. The captain tied his boat to a big post at the shore. He then led us to his house, about two hundred feet from the shore.

By now, it was about 9:00 p.m. He took us to a shed at the back of his house and said, "You can rest here tonight." He then left us with a bucket of drinking water, about five gallons.

The shed was about twelve feet by twelve feet, and hay covered the ground. Our feet were still wet and covered with sand. We all had a long day, so we just jumped up and slept on the haystack for the night. We woke up at dawn the next morning. We cleaned up and needed to change, to put on more civilized clothes, as we would be heading into Ha Tien and mingling among the Vietnamese population today.

By 9:00 a.m., we headed out to Ha Tien. Mom took us to meet up with Dad at a friend's house.

We all went to the Ha Tien market and headed to the bus station. Dad went to get the bus tickets to go to Ho Chi Minh City while Mom went to buy some food and drink. By 11:00 a.m., we got on to the bus and were heading to Ho Chi Minh

City. It was a five-hour bus ride, but to me, it was the best road trip I had in the last five years.

During the bus ride, I just learned from my dad that he was originally from Vietnam and his mom and all his siblings were still in Vietnam and we were heading to stay at one of my uncle's places in Ho Chi Minh City.

The twelve of us finally got to Ho Chi Minh City in the late afternoon, and we headed straight to my uncle's place. Honestly, arriving in Vietnam and heading straight to Ho Chi Minh City within one day was quite a lot for me to absorb, especially when we just came out of a war-ruined Cambodia. So I really did not know what to expect when I met with my newly discovered paternal relatives.

We got to my uncle's place around 6:00 p.m. We met with my cousins, The' and Thai', pronounced "Tei" and "Thai," for the first time. The' and Thai' were in their midteens, maybe twenty-two and twenty, respectively. The house had two rooms and a small kitchen outside. The total square footage was maybe eight hundred square feet, per my recollection.

The' and Thai' were very happy to see us, and I need to say they were so generous to allow us, twelve people, to stay in their house. And if not for the generosity of my cousin, we would not have a place to stay in Ho Chi Minh City that night. There was no way we could find a vacant place so soon. We had just entered Vietnam last night; nor could we afford the rent.

Now that the family, Grandma, uncles, and aunts had a place to stay for now, Dad took my brother and me to his hometown, Soc Trang, in Southern Vietnam. We were introduced to my paternal grandmother for the first time. My grandmother was in her seventies at the time. She was very happy and emotional to see us, likewise for us. We also went to another village not too far to visit my uncle (The' and Thai' parents).

Again, my uncle and family were very happy to see us and were very kind to us. After a weeklong trip, we returned to Ho Chi Minh City. We started to find a way to make a living in Vietnam, a new country. At the time, although the conditions in Vietnam were much better than Cambodia, it certainly was not a paradise. Vietnam's economy was under a lot of stress due to the US trade embargo, I was told. Many local people were unemployed, and there was slim chance for us to find work. So we became street hawkers. Basically, Uncle Chin would go out and buy some common and popular household items in bulk (soap, toothpaste, condensed milk, cigarettes, etc.), and we would try to sell it retail on the street.

We would pair up in a group of two. We had two groups and went out to a different street each day. Each group would bring out the merchandise by wrapping them in a square plastic tarp sheet. Once we found a suitable spot, we would lay open the square plastic tarp sheet on the sidewalk to display our merchandise for sale.

Selling merchandise on the street was not allowed by law. This was why we needed two people for each group, one person trying to conduct the business while the other looking out for hawker police. The hawker police patrolling the street in plain clothes could show up anytime during the day. I got paired up with my younger brother for this business operation.

If my brother, the looker, spotted a hawker police at a distance, he would call out, "Police!" I would then drop whatever I was doing, quickly grab the four corners of a square plastic tarp, and run away with the merchandise securely inside the tarp sheet. If the hawker police caught us, we would lose all our merchandise (this would be a devastating loss for us as we did not have much funds to start with) and maybe get sent to jail too because we were illegal residents after all. Once the police went away, we would return or find another spot to conduct our business. So you can see, it was a cat-and-mouse game every day.

After a few months of living in Ho Chi Minh City, it was clear we could not continue like this, as we could not make enough money to cover our expenses and we needed to do something new.

While in Vietnam, Dad secretly listened to the British Broadcasting Corporation (BBC) international radio broadcast every day, as this was the only reliable source for news without government censorship. He learned many Cambodians were escaping to Thailand. This prompted our family to consider Thailand as an alternative. We informed The' and Thai' that we were planning to go to Thailand in a few days and we were very grateful for their hospitality and generosity.

The' and Thai' were very excited to hear about this plan, to escape to Thailand. They told us many Vietnamese were also trying to get out of the country by boat. But going by boat was costly and very dangerous. Many people got killed on the sea. They asked if they could come along. We told them they were more than welcome to join us.

We told them although we knew Cambodia well, there would be risk and hardship they would need to endure. For starters, we needed to sneak back into Cambodia and prepare to trek the three hundred-kilometer journey on foot and sleep on the roadside, among other risks.

They said, "We are still young and fit. This is the best chance to get out of Vietnam we have. And we are willing to take a shot."

A few days later, we took a bus from Ho Chi Minh City to a city near the Cambodian border. After we arrived at the border city, we split up into two groups, group A and group B. The smaller group hopefully allowed us to cross the border without attracting unwanted attention. The plan was that each group would try to cross the border at a time. Each group would always stay together. But group A would continue, even if group B were held up. Similarly, group B would not stop for group A. Once we got into Cambodia, each group would continue heading west to Battambang, near the Thai border.

Group A had five people (Dad, Mom, my younger brother, Thai', and me). We walked to a border crossing and prepared to cross the bridge into Cambodia. As we were walking past a Vietnam border post to get onto the bridge, a Vietnamese soldier came out to stop my parents and Thai' while allowing my brother and me to continue.

You see, my brother and I looked like most Cambodians who had recently come out from the Khmer Rouge regime. Our skin was rough, and we looked malnourished. But my Dad, Mom, and Thai', with smooth and lighter skin color, certainly did not look like Cambodians who had worked under the hot sun for many hours.

My brother and I had no choice but to walk back and return to Vietnam. The guard called the border control office, who sent a jeep to take us to a Vietnamese border administration office about a kilometer away. They asked us to wait in a waiting room.

This office had a waiting room with one row of bench seats and a smaller office behind a counter. All the seats, tables, and counters were made of wood. The roof and wall were built using palm leaves knitted together to form a slap.

While we were waiting, Dad pulled out a piece of folded paper from his wallet. He inserted, to hide, the folded paper into the wall between the slaps of palm leaves. We knew we were in trouble. The only question was how to get out of this.

A man neatly dressed in uniform and shirt tucked in came to see us about an hour later. He must be the local border control officer who was in charge. He asked for an identification card. My dad, Mom, and Thai' handed over their laminated Vietnam ID cards. The man turned and looked at my brother and me, as if he also wanted to get our ID cards.

Dad told him, "They are my sons. They had been missing in Cambodia. We just found them recently, so they have no Vietnam IDs." My dad then handed the man a pack of cigarettes and asked for forgiveness.

The man went away with the ID cards and later returned. He asked Dad, "Why do you want to go to Cambodia?"

Dad replied, "We just found our missing two sons recently. They still have stuff in Cambodia. So we want to go and bring their belongings to Vietnam."

The man looked at each of us, one by one, as if he tried to look for body language and to gauge what Dad told him was true. He finally said, "Look, without paper approval, you three adults cannot go to Cambodia. But the two boys can go if they want to. And I would not report you this time. Please go back home to Ho Chi Minh City. And I don't want to see you again."

Dad said thank you to the officer, and we left the office as soon as we could. Now what next?

After we left the Vietnam border control office, Dad told us that piece of folded paper he inserted into the wall at the office was his public servant employee card. He said that if the border office were to find out he was a public servant, the officer would not let us off so easily, and we would be in big trouble. We would be sent to jail for sure. Wow, that was a close call!

By now, it was about noon local time. We went to buy some food to eat at a hawker store. Two men saw us, and they could tell we were not local. One man approached Dad and asked softly, "Do you guys want to cross the border to Cambodia?"

At first, Dad did not trust the man and said, "No."

The man pointed to a house across the street. "If you want some help to go to Cambodia, you can see me over there."

Before the man could walk away, Dad asked, "How much do you charge to get us across to Cambodia, and how to get over there?"

The man replied, "I have a boat, and I could take you all across." And he wrote the price on a piece of paper as a quote.

Dad looked at the quote and agreed with the price.

The man responded, "Ok, please come to rest at my place for today. We will leave at night tonight."

It was now about 1:00 p.m. We went to the man's house and rested. The man told us to hand over our bag packs so he could load them up onto the boat. Tonight at 8:00 p.m., he would come and bring us to his boat, and we would be off to Cambodia on the other shore.

We tried to rest for the afternoon at the man's house. About 4:00 p.m., the man came back and returned us the bags. He said, "Sorry, it is not good. We cannot go. I cannot bring you to Cambodia no more."

Dad was confused. "If tonight is not good, we can wait and try again tomorrow, correct?"

The man replied, "No, I don't want to do it anymore. Too risky. I don't want to get into trouble. Please leave now."

We believed these men were pirates. After we handed over our bags to them, supposedly to load the bags onto his boat, they must have searched our bags for any valuables (gold and cash). But they could not find any valuables in our bags. You see, many boat people who were escaping carried valuables with them. And these pirates would take the escapees to the open sea, kill them, throw them into the sea, and take away their valuables.

Luckily for us, we had no valuable stuff in our bag packs. So the men saw no reason or it was not worth it to kill us, I guess. Wow, we considered this another close call, and we got lucky for the second time in a day.

We walked away from the pirate's house and tried to figure out what to do next. It was now almost 5:00 p.m. We had a long day, and we did not have a clue what to do next. Where could we find a place to sleep tonight? And we were hungry. You see, this was a shanty border town. There was no Motel 6, Airbnb, or hotel of any kind in that border town in 1979. We decided to go to the market center to get some food and prepare to sleep on the sidewalk for the night.

We saw a hawker store not far away. We walked up and saw the hawker had three tables on the sidewalk. We sat down at one of the tables and ordered some food. A few minutes later, we saw two men come and sit down at a table next to us.

While we were waiting for our food, we heard the men were speaking in a local Chinese dialect with Kampot accent. Mom approached the men, introduced herself, and asked if they were from Kampot, Cambodia. Sure enough, the men were. Mom told them we were trying to get into Cambodia and asked for advice.

The men looked at Dad, Mom, and Thai' and said, "You don't look like Cambodians. You must have left Cambodia during the Khmer Rouge period and lived in Vietnam for some time."

Mom acknowledged and asked for advice. You see, during the difficult period, Cambodian people had this bonding and compassion to help one another. If you met a stranger and found out he was from your home city, chances are you would try to help one another as much as you can.

The man said, "I know of another border crossing not too far from here. They are not checking too strictly there. Maybe you can go and try there tomorrow."

My mom replied, "Thank you very much. Any other thing you think we need to do to improve our chances to cross the border?"

The man pointed to my brother and me. "Look at these two boys. Everyone can tell they are Cambodians, but you three adults are not. Your skin looks too smooth and too light. You two men had your shirts tucked in. No Cambodian does this. And your hair's too tidy."

The man continued, "Tomorrow, I would advise you two men not to shave. Don't comb your hair, and do not tuck your shirt in. Oh, one more thing, it is better to put on the oldest shirt you have and a darker color." He added, "By the way, do you plan to stay nearby for tonight?"

My dad replied, "Honestly, we don't know anybody in this town. We're still trying to find out where we can go to rest tonight."

The man offered help. "Tell you what. I have a friend who lives nearby. And if you come with me, maybe we can find a place for you to rest tonight."

And just like that, we found a place to sleep for the night. This is an example of why I feel my family and I had been so blessed, to meet generous and kind people each time we encountered obstacles.

After dinner, we joined the two men and walked to his friend's house. The friend was also originally from Kampot and was very kind to allow us to stay for the night. We chatted, shared our experiences, and got more advice to prepare for tomorrow's border crossing.

The next morning, we had breakfast and were about to say goodbye to our host. The house owner pulled out two old shirts in a dark color and gave them to my dad and Thai' to put on.

The man brought us to the local border crossing port. We got there at about 10:00 a.m. This port was situated at the southern end of the Mekong River, and the boat was taking passengers and goods between Vietnam and Phnom Penh. This port looked quite busy and bustling with people coming and going. Many of the passengers were Vietnamese and Cambodian traders, who were bringing household goods (fabric, soap, toothpaste, cigarettes, etc.) to sell in Cambodia. And more importantly, they did not check IDs or stop Vietnamese from entering Cambodia.

We saw a few medium-sized boats docked at the port, with engines still running and waiting to take passengers. Dad went to get the boat tickets. A few minutes later, Dad returned with the tickets. We said thank you and goodbye to our host, and he said good luck. And we walked down a walkway to the ticket check and got past with no incident this time.

The boat departed on time at 11:00 a.m. The boat had open-air ventilation and a roof to block the rain and sun. The boat had five rows of seats, and each row could seat four skinny people. The boat ride was very comfortable for me at the time. Every passenger got a front-row view to both sides of the Mekong River. The Mekong water on the Vietnam side did not look too clean. It was dark, cloudy, and even oily thanks to the pollution from all the boats' engines, garbage dumped along the riverbank, and runoff from the city drainage system.

Soon the boat entered Cambodia, and I was glad to see the Mekong water became clearer and cleaner as we moved forward and got deeper into Cambodia. I guess this was probably the only positive impact on the environment during the Khmer Rouge period. You see, for the last four years, there was literally no human present in Cambodia cities to cause any pollution along the Cambodia side of the Mekong River, and this allowed the Mekong to remain pristine still in 1979. All the flora and fauna on both sides of the river were untouched and beautiful. I am pretty sure, if we were to travel along the same waterway now in 2020, the health of the Mekong River in Cambodia would not be as pristine now, sadly.

We got to Phnom Penh about two hours later. Once we arrived, the capital city was still not fully operational. Remember, Cambodia was still recovering from the ruin by the Khmer Rouge. We saw many hawkers selling food and stuff on the street, and the currency in circulation was the Vietnamese currency, dong, because Cambodia still did not have an official currency.

We bought some food to eat and continued heading west. As we walked westward across the capital city, we saw similar ruin to the buildings as what we had witnessed in Kampot. Many buildings had doors and windows either damaged or pulled out completely. We saw some broken windows on the upper floor were boarded up with corrugated, galvanized steel panels or plastic panels. I guess people had to use whatever materials they had at the time, locally, to block the rain and the sun. We saw people walking up and down the street and some riding bicycles. Occasionally a military truck or a jeep was driving past. But we did not see any private cars or motorbikes on the road. We could see many buildings were occupied by people, but we did not see stores and shops.

We got to a town on the outskirts and west of Phnom Penh. Again no store was in sight. But we managed to buy some food from a street hawker using Vietnamese dong. We spent the night on the sidewalk outside Phnom Penh.

The next few days, we continued our journey, walking for five to six hours per day. There were miles and miles of beautiful and green paddy fields along both sides of the road, and the air was so fresh. Occasionally we saw a military truck heading our way. We would wave at the driver and try to get a ride. But most of the time, the truck did not stop. We normally would find a spot to rest at noon to escape the hot sun. On the road sometimes we bought some food to eat, mostly home-cooked food wrapped in banana leaves and carried out to sell by local hawkers. We would buy a few more wrapped food items to bring along as we did not know how far the next town was. For water, there was certainly no bottled water in Cambodia in 1979. But most farmhouses along the road had a water well, and we would ask the owner's permission to get some drinking water. And we would find a place along the roadside to sleep at night.

It was now about four weeks since we had heard the BBC news about Cambodian refugees entering Thailand. And we were in the middle of Cambodia, walking toward the Thai border. One night while we found a quiet spot to rest for the night, Dad turned on his shortwave radio to listen to the BBC. We heard how Thailand had used the military to push a few thousand Cambodian refugees back into Cambodia. This certainly was not good news for us because our plans and goals were to go to Thailand. But we were undeterred because we simply could not return to Vietnam or plan to stay in Cambodia.

So we continued to walk toward the Thai border and hope for the best. Each day we continued to walk westward and rest along the roadside, and Dad would listen to the BBC radio broadcast whenever he found a suitable spot and time. One evening while we were resting on the roadside, Dad turned on his radio, and we heard the news, "The US First Lady, Nancy Reagan, learned about the Cambodian refugee crisis at the Thai border while she was touring Southeast Asia. So she flew to the Thai border by helicopter to meet with some refugees on the ground. She promised to raise this human crisis issue at the United Nations Assembly in New York next week when she returned to the US. And she hoped the international community would contribute funds to support the Thai government to temporarily accept these refugees inside Thailand."

We continued our journey west on foot for a few more days. One evening Dad turned on his shortwave radio again, and the BBC announced that after the US First Lady delivered an emotional plea at the United Nations, many Western nations committed funds to support the Thai government's effort to house the Cambodian refugees. Now the Thai government had opened its border and was accepting new refugees.

This was indeed very good news and a big morale booster for our family. And we were now about a week away from getting to the Thai border. The timing could not be better. We woke up the next morning full of energy to continue our journey with new enthusiasm and hope.

We got to Kampong Chnang by the end of that day, and we found a place to rest at a three-way intersection under a big tree. Soon night fell, and we slept under the big tree. Around 3:00 a.m., we were all awakened in darkness by Dad loudly calling, "Thief! Thief! Thief!"

We saw a man running away with a bag in the dark. Dad tried to chase him down, but Mom said, "No, let him go. We don't know this place, and it can be dangerous." We found out the thief took a bag with my dad's radio in it.

Losing a radio at the time was a devastating blow for us, as this was the only window we had to the outside world. But somehow we always found a bright side to every ordeal.

Dad said, "Well, now that we got the good news about Thailand reopening the border, I guess we don't need the radio anymore. We can get a new one once we get to Thailand."

The next day, we were about to start walking. We saw a Vietnamese military truck heading our way and heading west. Dad waved, trying his luck, to ask for a ride.

And to our pleasant surprise, the truck stopped, and the driver asked, "Where are you heading?"

Dad replied, "We want to go to Battambang."

The driver said, "Ok, hop on to the back."

We quickly threw our bags onto the truck and climbed up on the back. And the truck started heading to Battambang.

Wow, we had waved at many different trucks over the last two weeks. But none had stopped for us. The timing was perfect. This ride to Battambang saved us at least one week of walking. You see, the Thai government had just reopened the border and was accepting new refugees. We needed to get into Thailand as soon as we could. Once too many refugees entered Thailand, at some point the Thai government might shut the border again. You just never know, and we could not miss this unique opportunity to enter Thailand.

This was the second time I got to travel on the back of a military truck. The first time was two years ago in 1977 during the Khmer Rouge period. At that time, the Khmer Rouge relocated our family, with twenty other families, to a new village. They loaded us onto the back of a truck like cattle. There were so many people that we all had to stand up throughout the journey. They pulled down the truck cover, and we traveled at night in complete darkness. We could not see where we were heading.

In contrast, this time we traveled during the day, and there was no covering to obstruct our view. Initially I stood up with both hands held onto the side guardrail for stability. As the truck moved ahead, I could feel the breeze blowing my hair, as if I were driving a convertible car, and I had a full view of the Cambodian landscape on both sides of the road.

But as the truck accelerated, the breeze became very chilly. So I decided to sit down. Since there was no seat, I put my backpack on the truck bed and sat on it. My backpack became my padded seat. Along the way, the kind driver made a couple of stops and picked up a few more passengers. We arrived at Battambang around noon.

The city looked in many ways similar to what we saw in Kampot. There were blocks of two- or three-story buildings on both sides of the road. Most of the buildings had been occupied by residents now. But we could tell the doors and windows had been damaged or torn down by the Khmer Rouge, as we saw the familiar scene of broken windows, now boarded up by the new residents, to prevent rainwater and sunlight from getting into the house. There were street hawkers busily trying to make a living by selling food and stuff on the street. We were new to Battambang, and we were trying to find some information, like how far is it from here to the Thai border and how to get to the Thai border. But there was no information booth in 1979, and neither cell phones nor Google Maps existed then. We would need to find opportunities to talk to people and try to gather the information we needed.

We saw a few street hawkers selling food on the street. We walked over, trying to buy some food to eat. I saw a hawker selling packages of MAMA Instant Noodle. And I did not know what MAMA Instant Noodle was.

You see, many Cambodians, including my brother and I, had been disconnected from the outside world for the last four years during the Khmer Rouge period. We never heard or had any knowledge about instant noodles. I assumed it must have come out to the market after 1975.

I inquired curiously, "What is MAMA Instant Noodle?"

The hawker explained, "See this package here. Each package has noodles for one person. It comes with a small pack of seasoning. You open the package, put the noodles into a bowl, open the small seasoning package, add the seasoning to the bowl, and then simply pour boiling water into the bowl. And in five minutes, your bowl of noodle soup is ready to eat."

The hawker added, "This is very good and popular, and it comes from Thailand." The hawker could tell my brother and I were excited about this MAMA Instant Noodle. He turned to Dad. "Do you want to get a few packs for the boys?"

My dad replied, "But we have no bowls. We just got here today."

The hawker explained, "No problem. Without water, you can also eat it like a snack."

As much as I would love to try this popular MAMA Instant Noodle, I told Dad, "No, we do not want it."

My brother and I assumed this MAMA Instant Noodle would be more expensive than local food because it was from Thailand. And we could not waste Dad's money on luxury items. (Yes, instant noodles were considered a luxury item for us at the time.) We needed to save and make the money last as long as we could, as we still had many days ahead.

You see, in 1979, Cambodia did not yet have import business with Thailand or any country. Cambodia did not even have its own currency. So all the Thai products on sale had to be smuggled in by foot. And these people were risking their lives to bring Thai products by foot from the Thai border to Battambang in Cambodia. They could be robbed, step on land mines, and get shot or caught in the gunfire between Vietnam and the Khmer Rouge in the forest. So meal for meal, MAMA Instant Noodle had to cost much more than the local steam rice cake.

We moved on to another vendor who was selling some local food, steam rice cake. Another vendor was selling baked bananas wrapped in sweet rice. We bought a couple of rice cakes and three baked bananas and sweet rice for lunch. We noticed in Battambang, in addition to using Vietnamese dong, Thai baht were also in circulation. I guess it made total sense as Battambang is closer to Thailand than Vietnam.

After lunch, Dad and Mom went for a walk around in Battambang to see if they could find more information on how to get to the Thai border effectively and safely, while we rested on the roadside. Dad and Mom returned about thirty minutes later and said Mom met her second cousin, whom Mom had not seen for many years. And her cousin had a place in Battambang.

So we packed up and went to meet her cousin. Another example of how lucky we are. We had been able to meet the right people at the right time. This no doubt helped make our journey to freedom easier.

We camped outside Mom's cousin's place for the night, as she had no spare room for guests inside. Mom told her we wanted to go to Thailand.

Mom asked her cousin, "Do you know which way or how to get to the Thai border?"

Her cousin said she did not know the way. But she saw many people coming to Battambang, and all were planning to head to Thailand. She pointed to a few families camped on the roadside. "You see those families over there? They just returned from Thailand. You can talk to them to get some information."

We saw a few families camped on the roadside across the street. Some had four people and others five. A few were just a young couple with infants. Dad went to talk to them, and he found out. These families were the first group of Cambodians who had entered Thailand about two months ago. They spent a few weeks in Thailand at makeshifts camp along the border, managed by the Thai military.

If you recall, about two weeks ago when the BBC news said the Thai military forcefully pushed out the Cambodian refugees back into Cambodia, unfortunately these were the families who were sent back into Cambodia. They told us the Thai army used military trucks to move a few thousand refugees to the border and asked them to walk into the forest back to Cambodia.

Most of the people refused to move initially. The Thai soldiers opened fire on refugees who refused to go back, killing hundreds of people on the spot. Thousands of refugees had no choice but to head into the forest and return to Cambodia. As people trekked through the forest, some walked off the trail to rest. Others went off trail to get water from the stream to drink, and many stepped on land mines and got killed. By unofficial estimate, because no official agency was there to count, about three thousand people were pushed into that forest, a few hundred people were shot by the Thai army, and a few hundred more people were killed by land mines in the forest.

Dad told them we heard the Thai government had reopened the border for Cambodian refugees after Nancy Reagan's speech at the United Nations Assembly.

One man told Dad, "We are not going back to Thailand, no matter what. My family has suffered enough. I lost my father and a brother. They stepped on land mines when they tried to fetch some water for the family to drink."

Another man said, "We want to give it another try, to go back to Thailand. And we plan to leave tomorrow."

For us, our minds were already set. We did not plan to stay in Cambodia, and we must not go back to Vietnam. Dad asked the man if we could join his family.

The man gladly replied, "Yes, we can walk together."

The man turned to my Cousin Thai'. "I noticed he did not speak and he does not look like Cambodian. He is Vietnamese, correct?"

My dad acknowledged, "Yes, he is my nephew, and he is Vietnamese. But he can speak some Cambodian."

The man warned, "When we walk through the forest, we will encounter some Khmer Rouge soldiers on the trail. The Khmer Rouge soldier would look for Vietnamese. And they would kill all Vietnamese and anyone associated with the Vietnamese if they spot one."

You see, since Vietnam kicked out the Khmer Rouge, many Cambodians considered Vietnamese as liberators, including my family. But the Khmer Rouge considered all Vietnamese as enemies, including civilians.

Although most of the Vietnamese refugees got out of Vietnam by boat, this is the reason they were called boat people. A small number of Vietnamese also tried their luck by entering Thailand via Cambodia. My cousin The' and Thai' were among them.

The man added, "For my family's sake, please don't call my family or me if the Khmer Rouge spots you. For your own sake, do not open your mouth to say a word when we walk in the forest." The man continued, "I really mean it. Keep your mouth shut. Some Khmer Rouge speaks Vietnamese too. And when he spots a suspect Vietnamese, he would talk to you in Vietnamese to see your reaction."

We stayed on the roadside in front of my mom's cousin's house. Another family was camped next to us. Soon night fell, and before we went to sleep, Dad said, "Tomorrow we will follow the man to walk to the border and into Thailand. The man said there would be quite a few people trekking to Thailand too. And here is our plan. We will split into two groups, group A (Dad and me) and group B (Mom, my brother, and Thai')."

Just in case we got split up for whatever reason, we would never walk back. If group A got to Thailand first and did not see group B, group A must not return, but group A would wait inside the Thai border for a day. If group B did not show up after one day, group A needed to move.

"Go and move ahead. No need to wait."

Thai' looked at us (Dad, Mom, my brother, and me) and said, "And if the Khmer Rouge stop me, please do not turn back for me."

Dad quickly chimed in, "No, we could not do this to you. How am I going to face my brother or your dad?"

A man who camped next to us overheard the conversation, and he offered to help. "Look, here is a used traditional Cambodian scarf. If you wrap this around your neck during the walk tomorrow, this would make you look like a Cambodian Chinese and not Vietnamese. Good luck."

Thai' said thank you to the man for his kindness and help.

Dad concluded, "We have a long day tomorrow. Let's go to sleep now."

The next morning, we followed the man and his family and headed out west at sunrise. The man said we hoped to get to the border town by noon. This way we would have some time to rest. We walked past miles and miles of beautiful rice paddy fields on both sides of the road. We also saw different groups of families walking in the same direction. We assumed they were just like us, heading to Thailand.

We got to the border town about noon. I could not remember the name of that small town. But I could recall we saw a forest on the west side of the town.

The man told Dad, "We will rest here this afternoon. We will be heading into the forest tonight. And it will take about eight hours, by foot, to get into Thailand." The man explained, "It is not safe to walk in the forest during the day because the Khmer Rouge and Vietnamese soldiers are on patrol during the day. And they could be shooting at each other any time, and we do not want to get caught in the fighting."

We and many families rested on the roadside in this small town that afternoon. Soon night fell, and by about 9:00 p.m., the small town was quiet, and there was no traffic of any kind at all at night.

The man said, "Ok, we are heading out now."

With a bag pack filled with two pairs of clothing, a Cambodian scarf or towel, and some rice cake, we followed the man and headed out west. From the small town, we walked along a narrow road under the moonlight, with no streetlight, for about thirty minutes.

We then entered a trail barely wide enough for an ox cart to pass. The trail had not been maintained for some time, as there were tall and thick brush on both sides. But it looked like the trail had been frequented by people or had heavy foot traffic because the ground was firm and it was not covered with overgrown grasses.

There were about forty of us forming a human train entering the trail. Our family was in the second half of this human train. There were about twenty people ahead of me. Dad and I walked side by side. Mom and my brother were also walking side by side. Thai' walked right behind them. There were a few people following behind Thai'. There was no rain, and the temperature was cool at night, perfect for trekking.

I noticed a few mosquitos and bugs flying around, but it did not bother us, well, at least not me. Everyone was moving at a good pace, and we continued to trek quietly under the moonlight for about an hour. Along the trek, we encountered a group of young men walking in the opposite direction (from Thailand to Cambodia), and each man carried a big bag pack on their back, filled with Thai products.

Since these men carried heavy loads, we moved to the right to give way for them to pass. These men were bringing Thai products to sell in Battambang. They were risking their lives on every trip they made. I assumed the money must be quite good.

We followed the trail as it turned right into the forest. The trees were about twenty feet tall, and the forest was so thick, such that the moonlight could barely shine through. We continued to trek and follow the winding trail in darkness, barely able to see the person in front.

But we could not turn on any lighting because light might attract unwanted attention. We followed the group and continued to push forward for some three hours into the journey, still in the deep forest. We suddenly heard several gunshots in front of us, followed by people screaming, "Robbery! Robbery!"

Everybody quickly dug down and crawled off the trail to hide. Some people went to the left, and others went to the right, in the forest.

We could tell this trail had been frequented by many Cambodian people traveling to and from Thailand. Some people were trying to escape to Thailand as refugees. Others were traders or porters trying to make some money by bringing goods from Thailand to sell in Cambodia. Both groups would carry valuables (gold and cash) with them. This naturally attracted robbers, like they said. When there is prey, there will be predators.

Back to the forest, my dad held my hand tightly, as if he did not want to lose me in the woods. We sat down on the ground and hid in the thick brush and darkness. We could hardly see one another, and the place was so quiet that I could hear my dad breathing. I could tell there were two other people who sat about two meters away, or five feet, from me. But I had no idea who they were. But I could not speak or ask them. If you speak, the robbers would hear you and know someone was hiding there. I simply assumed the two people were my mom and my brother. We laid down on the ground.

About forty minutes later, in darkness, my dad pulled me up slowly, but he did not say a word because we did not want to draw any attention. Still hiding in the tall brush, occasionally we saw people walking in groups of three or four, in darkness, but we could not tell who they were. Were they the same people we had been trekking with, a new group of people, or the robbers? We quietly moved closer to observe the people moving on the trail for a few minutes. We saw men, women, and some children, so we figured they were not robbers. Like us, they were people trying to go to Thailand.

We slowly moved back onto the trail when there were no people. We started moving forward in silence, with my dad still holding my hand tightly, as we were still walking in the Red Zone. (Red Zone referred to the area where most of the robberies occurred. This zone was lawless because neither the Cambodian government nor the Thai government was controlling this area in the forest. So it was a Wild West.)

We finally exited the thick forest and headed out into the prairies. This time we could see people on the trail more clearly under the moonlight, but we were not out of the Red Zone yet. So we all still moved forward quietly. As we moved forward, we could see the moonlight slowly disappear, and it was quickly replaced by the sunrays on our back.

About twenty minutes later, daylight arrived, and we could see people much clearer now. I looked in front. I saw a couple walking. I turned around. I saw a man and a teenage boy walking side by side. But I could not see my mom, my brother, or Thai'. I looked at Dad.

Dad continued to hold my hand and said, "Don't worry. Let's continue to move forward. Maybe they are ahead of us."

Soon we saw three Khmer Rouge soldiers standing on the trail in front of me with AK-47s. They were standing on the trail and did not bother us. I guess they could tell we were not Vietnamese.

My father and I continued to trek for another hour, and we saw a half-dozen soldiers in green camouflage uniforms. These soldiers were standing on the trail, holding American M16 guns. At first, I thought they were Thai soldiers because we know both the Khmer Rouge and Vietnamese mostly carried AK-47s, likely Chinese made.

But as we moved closer, I heard they were instructing people to move forward in Cambodian. I did not want to ask questions because I still did not know whether we had exited the Red Zone or not. We continued to move forward, and then we came to what looked like a huge campsite under the trees in the forest.

As my dad and I entered this campsite, we looked around and tried to find out more information about this site. Are we in Thailand yet? Who are the paramilitary? Can we stay here? Or do we have to continue to move?

We learned during that time, there were two groups of Cambodian forces fighting the Vietnamese along the border: first the Khmer Rouge supported by communist China and the second group called Cambodian Paramilitant. In Cambodian language, "para" referred to the green camouflage military uniform. Therefore we called this group Para Group, short for Paramilitant Group. We did not know who was leading this paramilitant group. Anyway, we just wanted to get to Thailand, and we did not care about their politics.

This campsite we just entered was under the control of a Cambodia paramilitant. The site had several rows of streets with huts on both sides, like a chessboard. Several streets went from east to west, and several roads cut across them, going from north to south. There were several hundred huts on both sides of the streets. The walls and roofs of these huts were built using plastic tarp sheets. And at least two to three thousand people were living there, some permanently and others temporarily. They even had hawkers selling home-cooked meals (steam rice and noodle soup) or some Thai cookies and snacks. To sum up, this site looked like a huge California state fair under the big redwood forest, if there were such an event.

My dad and I entered this campsite at about 8:00 a.m., and we were extremely thirsty, hungry, and exhausted. So the first order of business was to find some water to drink and food to eat. We walked along the road and saw a few hawker stores selling steam rice and other food. The money in circulation here was Thai baht. We also saw a money changer booth. We went to sell one ounce of gold for Thai baht and use it to buy food.

Dad asked the woman, "How much is a bowl of rice?"

I could not remember exactly how much a bowl of steam rice cost in Thai baht. After all, it was almost forty years ago. But I remembered it was quite expensive. For example, at the time, one ounce of gold could only buy about fifty meals. Compared to today's rate, one ounce of gold can easily buy two hundred meals if a meal costs US$20. As you can see, a meal costs four times as much.

We later learned the paramilitant group controlled and ran this campsite. The group made money on every business transaction on this site. You see, these hawkers who set up stores in this market needed to pay protection fees to the Cambodian paramilitary. Thai traders brought most of the food (rice, meat, vegetable, etc.) to sell to these hawkers. The Thai traders also needed to pay protection fees to the Cambodian paramilitant group. On top of that, it was risky to do business here because fighting could erupt anytime without warning. And the hawkers could lose everything, including their lives, in a flash.

We walked ahead to check the price at different stores. Dad finally decided to buy two meals. We finished the food in no time but were still hungry. But we could not afford any more, as we needed to save our money for the day ahead.

After the meal, we realized Mom, my brother, and Thai' were not with us. Dad and I walked back to the entrance of the campsite we entered earlier. He told me to wait here and look out for Mom, my brother, and Thai' while he was going to check out this place, to see if he could find out more information and prepare a place to rest tonight.

Dad returned about two hours later. I told him there was no sign of Mom, my brother, or Thai' yet. We found a spot to sit down on the ground and yet were able to keep an eye on the traffic at the entrance. Dad said he met one of his former students at the far side of the camp. (My dad was a teacher for many years, so he had many former students in Cambodia.) His friend had a unit on this site, and we could go there to sleep tonight if we needed to.

We sat and waited at the camp entrance for the whole day, yet there was no sign of them. By 5:00 p.m., my dad asked me to stay here while he went to his student's unit to cook dinner. (It would be much cheaper compared to buying meals from the hawkers since we needed to spend our money very wisely.)

After the sunset, Dad came to bring me back to his student's unit for dinner. As I reentered the site, this place was lit up with so many lights, like a night out at a summer fairground, and the street was bustling with hawkers selling food and people walking up and down. We went straight to the unit to have dinner. She cooked some steam rice, and my dad prepared a simple cabbage soup with salt and nothing else, no meat or chicken. That bowl of steam rice with cabbage soup was the best meal I ever had in my life. Almost forty years later, I could still vividly remember the sweet taste of that cabbage soup. (When you are starving, all food tastes amazingly good.)

After dinner, we asked her how to get to Thailand. She told us. We were still inside the Cambodian forest. Her husband had joined the paramilitant group, and she had been living here for six months now. This camp acted like a funnel. The paramilitant group was controlling the people in and out of this camp quite effectively. The para soldiers we saw on the trail were counting how many people were entering the camp per day. Many of the huts in the camp were for rent and run by paramilitant families, and they had capacity for six hundred people. The group normally saw two to three hundred people entering the camp per day. The migrants needed food and a place to stay during their transition through the camp. The militant group ran all the businesses on the site.

Once the number of people entering this site reached capacity, the para group would call the Thai military, about ten kilometers from here, to send buses to pick up the migrants to become refugees in Thailand. These buses sent from

Thailand to pick up Cambodian refugees were funded by the United Nations Refugee Relief Agency. But the paramilitants sold bus tickets to everyone who needed a bus ride into Thailand. I assume the Thai also made a cut from this. So you can see that this was quite a moneymaking operation. In all fairness, my dad's student did not make money from us. She gave us a big discount. And we are grateful for her hospitality and guidance.

Dad told her we would wait one more day for my mom, my brother, and Thai'. If they still did not show up tomorrow, we planned to head into Thailand, with or without them.

She said, "Ok, I will get you the bus tickets whenever you need to go."

We went to bed soon. She told us in most cases, new people arrived between sunrise and noon. So it would be better we go to wait for them at dawn.

The next morning, we woke up at 5:00 a.m. and had a simple breakfast. We hurriedly went back to the camp entrance before sunrise to look for Mom, my brother, and Thai'. My dad and I sat down alongside the trail and waited for them patiently. We saw many different people walking into the camp, some in groups of two, three, or four. But still there was no sign of Mom, my brother, or Thai'.

By 9:00 a.m., after some three hours of waiting with still no sign of them, I could tell Dad was increasingly worried, as he kept walking up and down and puffing his cigarette. I knew we had a plan and had supposedly prepared for the worst if we got split up and they didn't show up. We needed to go to Thailand, no matter what happened. But if something did not turn out well and you had to decide, it still could be pretty tough.

As you could see, during and after the robbery that night, many things could have easily gone wrong:

- They could have gone off the trail too far and got lost in the jungle, because they could not find their way back to the trail we were on.
- They could have gone off the trail, stepped on land mines and killed.
- They could have gone off the trail and were walking on a different trail headed to a different camp along the Thai border (we learnt later there were 3 different camps along the Cambodian-Thai border)
- The three got split up and only one or two of them showed up.

But honestly, I was not sure what I would do if my brother did not show up (no offense to Mom or Thai'). You see, my younger brother and I had been through a lot together in the past nine years. I was not sure I could move on, a final step, without my brother.

After walking up and down while waiting for a few hours, Dad decided to sit down and rest under a tree. He leaned against the tree on his back. I guessed he must have been tired. He told me to keep an eye on the trail and not to wander too far. I was drawing something for fun on the ground with a dead tree branch I picked up to kill time while keeping my eye on the trail every now and then.

Occasionally I saw people emerge from the shadow of the forest, sometimes individually or other times in small groups, onto the trail and head in my direction and toward the camp entrance. About midday, finally I spotted my brother about a hundred meters away as he walked out from the forest and headed my way.

I dropped my drawing stick, jumped up excitedly, waved, and called, "Long! I am here!" I called again, "Long! I am here!" (Long is my younger brother's name.)

My brother spotted me, and we ran toward one another. As I was running toward my brother, I saw my mom and Thai' following behind, each with a walking stick. As my brother and I hugged each other, I noticed he carried two backpacks. So I off-loaded one from him. Like that, we reunited. We took them to Dad's student's hut to get much-needed drinks and food. We rested in the camp for one more night.

Seven

Refugee in Thailand

The next morning, we all woke up at dawn as we were very excited that we were going to enter Thailand today. Mom cooked some breakfast. After breakfast, my dad's student took us to take the bus. She walked us to a gate on the north side of the camp. There were a gate and a guard post. We said thank you and goodbye to our host at the exit gate, and we entered a trail with tall trees on both sides. We followed the trail and walked for about ten minutes. We emerged on the other side of the woods. There, we saw some people already standing in line. They told us we should wait here for the bus. They added the bus was supposed to come in about thirty minutes. More and more people joined the line while we were waiting for the bus.

Soon we saw three buses coming, and as the buses get closer, we saw a sign on the bus windscreen that said "UNHCR and Red Cross International."

We knew what Red Cross meant, but none of us knew what UNHCR stood for. Anyway, we were so happy to see the Red Cross sign, as this meant we were now being helped. As the buses moved closer and stopped, a man came out of the first bus with a handheld microphone.

"Good morning everyone, I work for the UNHCR." He added, "UNHCR stands for United Nations High Commissioner for Refugees. Please get on the bus, and we will take you to Camp Khao I Dang."

One by one, we got on to the coach bus. I was so excited, as this was my first time to get on a coach bus. The bus interior was very clean with air-conditioning and nicely padded seats. All these features were new and very luxurious to me. Soon the buses started to head out and travel on the dirt road for about ten minutes. Then the buses turned right onto a road, and within minutes we saw a road sign in Thai.

One man called out excitedly when he saw the sign board in Thai, "We are in Thailand!"

We followed him excitedly, "We are now in Thailand!"

The bus driver acknowledged over his microphone, "Yes, you are now in Thailand."

The buses continued to move forward, and about thirty minutes later, the buses slowed down, turned right, exited the main road, and stopped at a checkpoint guarded by Thai soldiers. Through the bus side window, I saw a huge open space. It was surrounded by barbed wire fence and facing a big mountain on the far side. At the camp entrance, a few big tents were set up as office and meeting spaces with bench counters and bench chairs.

I also saw big signs with **UNHCR** and **Red Cross** displayed on the wall. And there were about twenty people, men and women, behind the bench counters, as if they were waiting to see people.

The driver told us, "We have arrived at Camp Khao I Dang. This camp was just opened last week, and you may get off the bus now." We said thank you to the driver as we alighted the bus.

A Cambodian man, maybe a volunteer worker, welcomed us to Camp Khao I Dang. He gave us a brief introduction. "Camp Khao I Dang is situated at the foothill of Khao I Dang mountain. The site has approximately 2.3 square kilometers. This is a new refugee camp officially opened last week. It is funded and managed by UNHCR and with Thai government support. Please go to the counter for registration."

At the registration counter, we were given a two-page form to complete. We needed to fill in basic information like name, age, sex, relationship for each family member, and country of origin. The registration form had a box for each family to fill in, which country they would like to go, and if the family had any preference. At the end of the form, there was a list of countries that may accept refugees under humanitarian policy: United States, France, and other Western countries.

United States and France were the countries of choice for many Cambodian refugees because of the US involvement in the Cambodian civil war and France's status as a former colonist. My dad put down we would like to go to the United States and said we were also willing to go to any country.

After registration, another Red Cross worker came and took us, a group of about a hundred people, to the plot of land assigned to us to build our houses. The campsite was divided into many blocks, and each block was supposed to house about ten thousand refugees. Since we were the early arrivals, the second week of opening, we were assigned to block two, group three.

As we walked to the plot of land designated to block number two, we saw a stack of building materials and tools already delivered to each block for us to build our new house. The building materials provided were big bamboo for posts, medium-size bamboo for beams and structures. There was a plastic tarp sheet and knitted palm leaf for walls and roofs.

The men from the same group worked together to build houses in a row. Then each house was sectioned based on the size of a family. We had five people and were given a space about the size of a standard living room, or four hundred square feet. Basically each house would have a room and one big bed for sleeping. The bed was also built using bamboo. Thanks to the Khmer Rouge, many Cambodian men now knew how to build a house quite well.

First, we would dig holes, each two feet deep, for the posts. We tied or nailed the bamboos together to build a frame for the house. We used plastic tarp sheets for the first layer of the roof to prevent rainwater from going through. We then laid knitted palm leaves on top of the plastic tarp, which would keep the house cool. The same knitted palm leaves materials were also used for walls. The house construction at Camp Khao I Dang was like walking in a park compared to what we had to do during the Khmer Rouge period. Here, all the building materials were delivered pre-cut to size, and we got everything we needed.

A group volunteer leader was identified to help with the distribution of food and basic needs for ten families. A group leader would represent the ten families and be the key interface between the group and the UNHCR staffer. Each family would take turns to help the group leader with the basic tasks of distributing food and water, block cleaning, and so forth.

For the first few weeks, we went to the registration office to see if we could find Grandma and other family members among the new refugees arriving daily. If you recalled, we split up into two groups when we got to the Vietnam-Cambodia border about six weeks ago, and we had gone separate ways. We had not been in touch since.

About a week later, we were so happy to find Grandma, Uncle Chin, and others at the registration office. It was great to see everyone had made it to Thailand safely. This was the first time my cousins, The' and Thai', had been separated for this long. So I could tell Thai' was so happy to see his brother had also made it safely to Camp Khao I Dang. Grandma's group was assigned to block seven, if I recall correctly.

To give you a sense of how many Cambodians left the country after the fall of the Khmer Rouge in 1979, within one month from opening, Camp Khao I Dang accepted some 84,000 refugees, on average 3,000 people per day.

Since the refugee camp, by design, was not meant to house people permanently, there was no running water system, electricity line, or sewage system installed. All the water needed to be hauled in by many tank trucks daily to support life in the camp. Each person would get about five gallons of water per day for all their needs (drinking, cooking, washing, and all cleaning).

You probably thought I had a typo with five gallons of water per day per person. No, it was not a typo. We were actually getting five gallons of water per day per person. It was not easy to live with five gallons of water per day. But we also knew the UNHCR, the Red Cross, and many volunteers had sacrificed their personal life and worked tirelessly to support us in this camp. So we really appreciated their kindness and generosity.

Anyway, we learned to manage and improvise. People dug a trench behind each house to collect rainwater from the roof using plastic tarp sheets. Most trenches could hold thirty to fifty gallons of water.

About eight weeks after its opening, Camp Khao I Dang had reached maximum capacity at 160,000 people. So no more new refugees were coming in. Before the Khmer Rouge, many Cambodians, including our family, had never thought about leaving our home country, let alone becoming a refugee. Now many Cambodian refugees hoped to migrate to a new country to start a new life and, for the younger generation, to have a better future. This was because our own country had been ruined by civil war and run by incapable leaders whose disastrous economic policies killed millions, specifically communism.

As a young child during the Khmer Rouge period, many Cambodian kids and I were taught that for hundreds of years Cambodians had been robbed and suppressed by the French colonists and Western capitalists (France, United States, etc.).

To me, the colonial history might be true. But it was in the past. All I had seen and experienced was, in modern Cambodia, Cambodians fighting and killing one another. The country was left to ruin, and generations of kids were robbed of opportunities to go to school and a chance to get a better life. And now when many Cambodian refugees like me were most vulnerable, I personally saw that the countries willing to help us and give us a new home were all Western capitalist countries.

Since we all hoped and planned to settle in one of the Western countries and we knew many countries used the English language, everyone would try to learn English to improve their chances to get accepted by the immigration interview and to be able to succeed in a new country.

Although there was no official school inside the camp, many people were trying to learn English privately at home. People who know English could also make some money inside the camp by giving private lessons. My first English book was called *The Essential English for Foreign Students, Volume One*, by Addison Wesley Longman. This book was very popular among English learners in Vietnam and Cambodia.

Since we could not afford to buy a new book, Dad bought a used one from his friend for us. His friend had completed volume one, and he had moved on to volume two. My brother and I were very excited to have our first English book. Our first English lesson was from my cousin The'. The' had learned English at college in Saigon, Vietnam. He would come to teach us English about once a week. Also Mom was teaching my brother and me some Mandarin Chinese inside the camp. So we were learning two languages inside the camp, and it was also a good time for us to catch up on the years we missed school.

Unfortunately my cousins The' and Thai' needed to move to a Vietnamese section of the camp about two months after we settled in the camp, all this because of some racial tension between the Cambodians and Vietnamese. You see, initially all the refugees were assigned to the blocks and houses based on arrival date, not country of origin. So there were a few Vietnamese living among many Cambodians.

At the time, a majority of Khao I Dang refugees were Cambodians, and there were only a couple of thousand Vietnamese. With any big group of population, there would be some tension or small issues. But a few Cambodian bad apples used all kinds of excuses to create tension, to gang up and threaten the small Vietnamese group. The Vietnamese rightfully reported to the camp authority, and they decided to move all the Vietnamese to one section of Camp Khao I Dang, segregated them from the Cambodians, before this tension got out of hand. But this also did not eliminate the tension completely. Soon the Thai authority relocated all the Vietnamese refugees to a different campsite. So my two cousins, The' and Thai', sadly moved away from us.

After The' departure, our English lessons were put on hold. Fortunately the Red Cross also offered English lessons to the refugees in the camp. My brother and I would spend our day looking for the date, time, and open slots for English lessons. Many of the teachers were volunteers from different Western countries. They came to teach at the camp for a few weeks at a time.

As you can imagine, demand for English classes always exceeded supply. So it was not easy to get a slot. I managed to get maybe a lesson once per week, if I were lucky. And in many cases, each time I got a different teacher who came from a different country. Since this was my first exposure to English, it was not easy to follow teachers with so many different accents at the time.

I recalled my first lesson was with Mrs. Kovac of California. She was good, and the lesson was clearly understood. But two weeks later, I got into a class, and the teacher was from Scotland. And I could not understand a single word he was saying. Since there were at least eighty students, there was no chance for me to ask any questions.

About once a month, we had representatives from different Western countries coming to Camp Khao I Dang to interview the lucky families for resettlement purposes. I did not know what criteria they were using to select the lucky families. But we learned there was a three-step process:

1. Whenever a country representative wanted to interview a refugee for resettlement, they would post the name of the lucky family on the notice board. Normally they would post names of the lucky families one week in advance, with specific dates and times for the interview. So the camp notice boards were normally crowded with people eager to find their name on the list.

2. Next was the face-to-face interview. Once a family name was posted, the family would have to show up for a one-hour face-to-face interview through an interpreter. If you missed your interview, you would have to wait for the next cycle, and nobody knew if you would ever get a second chance. Most refugees could not afford to miss this opportunity.

3. The final phase was the health screening. This was the most important phase because you cannot move on if you failed this one.

My dad would go to scan the notice board daily, hoping our name would show up as soon as possible. But not every country could accept refugees regularly. There were immigration quotas and procedures they needed to follow. In many cases, a country could only take a few hundred people per quarter. And there were 160,000 refugees in Camp Khao I Dang. If our name did not appear this month, we simply needed to wait for our turn.

About four months after we settled in Khao I Dang, the first list of lucky families was put up to be interviewed by the United States. Unfortunately our names were not on the list. We knew there was nothing we could do but wait. We stayed positive and focused our energy on trying to learn more English and Mandarin Chinese.

Although the UNHCR and the Red Cross had provided us with food (rice and canned food) and water, the people can only eat canned food for so long. After a few weeks of canned food, people needed to have fresh vegetables and fruits and some basic household items like clothes, soap, and so forth. A few enterprising refugees saw the demand and business opportunity. You see, the Thai military managed everything coming into the camp.

A few entrepreneur refugees somehow were able to get the Thai soldiers to bring them some vegetables and fruits to sell. I guess the Thai soldiers took a cut by selling these items to the men. Initially the men put some vegetables and fruits on sale in front of his house. And they were sold out like hotcakes. The men got the Thai soldiers to bring in more goods, and still they could not catch up with the demand. Within a few weeks, a whole block was turned into a marketplace with many hawker stands within the camp. They were selling vegetables, fresh fruits, clothes, and household items. Soon other stores also popped up to provide English lesson classes, hair salons, and fortune-tellers among them.

It turned out fortune-teller services were also in high demand. You see, emotionally, life in the refugee camp can be lonely and stressful because barbed wire surrounded the camp. All the refugees needed to stay inside the camp all the time, and there was not much to do inside the camp, with no employment, school for the kids, church, television, and so forth.

Being a refugee does not guarantee a visa to migrate to a new country. On the contrary, all refugees could be repatriated anytime when the UNHCR or the host country decided to close the camp for whatever reason. Many refugees hoped they could go to settle in a new country as soon as possible because we had given up everything to make the journey to Thailand. In our case, my parents gave up their jobs in Vietnam and used up all their savings. Also, we wanted to be independent and able to support ourselves as quickly as we could. My parents hoped we could go to a new country soon so my brother and I would be able to go to school as we had already missed school in the past nine years due to civil war and the Khmer Rouge.

Many refugees hoped to see their names on the notice board as soon as possible. It can be straining psychologically if they kept seeing other lucky families were selected, month after month, but their name was not. Our family stayed in the camp for twenty months. You could imagine the anxiety my parents had to endure each month. So mentally, life in the camp could be very tough, and people were so eager to have a glimpse of their future, even it may be just an illusion. So fortune-tellers could be very helpful for stress relief because they gave people hope, a light at the end of a tunnel.

The UNHCR and many volunteers knew life in the camp was not easy and could be lonely. They tried to make our lives a bit more interesting by providing one movie night per month. They put up a huge white screen on a big, open space inside the camp. They played some old movies via a projector and loudspeakers. This indeed was very popular for all the refugees. People would sit on a dirt floor in rows in front of the screen to enjoy foreign movies with subtitles.

I remembered most were French movies and in French. Maybe they assumed many Cambodians would understand French. Since there were many more people and limited space in front of the screen, some people would sit at the back of the screen also to enjoy the movie. I did that a few times, and it was not too bad. You just saw all the action in the opposite direction.

In addition to the international organization, we also had a local Thai charitable group who came to visit us and bring in donations for refugees. A Thai-Chinese newspaper learned that there were Cambodian Chinese among the refugees in Camp Khao I Dang. They brought in many used clothes donated by the Thai-Chinese community for the refugees. We were very touched by their kindness and generosity.

My dad was one of the camp community leaders who went to meet the Thai-Chinese visitors. My dad knew he had an old friend who lived in Bangkok for many years. But he had lost contact with his friend. All he got was his friend's name. My dad asked the representative from the Thai-Chinese newspaper if they could help him locate his friend in Bangkok. They agreed to put an ad in a Bangkok daily newspaper.

Two weeks later, my dad's friend drove all the way from Bangkok, some two hundred miles away, to visit my dad at the camp. He brought in many clothes and household items for us. I called him Mr. Kiet. Mr. Kiet had been very kind to support us during our twenty-month stay in the Thai refugee camp. I want to take this opportunity to say thank you to Mr. Kiet for his kindness.

About a year after we settled in Camp Khao I Dang, I had a chance to see a dentist for the first time in my life. I really did not know what to expect. I could not remember why I went to see the dentist. I did not have toothaches. Maybe it was one of the general dental checkups the camp offered to every kid.

I vividly remember the dentist introduced himself, "I am Doctor Brown." I recalled this because it was an easy name, as it was also the name used in my English book (*The Essential English for Foreign Students*). Anyway, he asked me to open my mouth wide. He looked at my teeth.

The next thing he said was, "You never visited a dentist before, did you?"

I replied through an interpreter, "No, sir. I never had toothaches."

He looked at me and smiled. He told me my teeth were good and he found no cavities. But my teeth needed a thorough cleaning. So he gave me a deep clean. I said thank you very much to Dr. Brown at the end and said goodbye.

Soon it was May 1981. We had been living in the refugee camp for about eighteen months. There were rumors in the camp that next month a few countries would come to interview families for resettlement. For thirty days, we waited anxiously and prayed we could find our names on the lucky list this time.

Soon June arrived, and the names list was posted on the board. Dad went to scan the notice board like any other day. But this time, our prayer was answered. He saw our name on the list to be interviewed by New Zealand next week. Dad rushed home excitedly to tell us the good news.

Mom asked, "Where is New Zealand?"

We knew nothing about New Zealand, but we were still very happy and looking forward to our interview next week. For the next few days, we tried to find out any information about New Zealand. Dad managed to get a printed world map in black and white. Since we knew the countries that were willing to accept refugees for resettlement were mostly Western countries, we searched for New Zealand in Western Europe on the map. After ten minutes of combing every indexed block on Western Europe, New Zealand was still nowhere to be found.

We then moved to North America. We saw the United States and Canada, but still we could not find New Zealand. We looked at each other puzzlingly. Maybe Dad got the wrong spelling, or maybe it was The Netherlands? My brother and I went back to check the name on the notice board again.

Yes, New Zealand was spelled correctly. We divided the map into four blocks (top left, top right, bottom left, and bottom right), and each person started scanning each block on the black-and-white map. My brother got the bottom right, and he spotted New Zealand in the South Pacific Ocean, next to Australia and many Polynesian islands.

The next question: what language do they speak in New Zealand? We hoped they spoke English, else the English lessons my brother and I had taken would be wasted. It would have been very useful if we had Google and Google Maps then. There was no questionnaire list we could find to prepare for the interview. The best I could do was read my English book and rehearse a few simple questions and answers with my brother.

About a week later, we also learned that Grandma and other family names were to be interviewed by the United States the following week.

Soon our interview date arrived. We went to the front office for our interview with the New Zealand immigration staffer. The four of us were nervous and excited at the same time as we sat in the waiting room. Soon a nice lady came out and called our names. We stood up, and she introduced herself as Diane Johnson.

We were seated inside a room. She turned to my brother and me and asked, "How are you boys?"

I stood up proudly, also a bit nervous. "I am fine. Thank you. How are you?"

She replied, "Very good. I see you have been learning English."

I showed her my English book. "Yes, I practiced with my younger brother."

She basically asked and validated our names and Mom and Dad's occupation against our registration form. She then turned to my dad and asked, "I see you had been a school deputy principal. What kind of job would you like to do when you go to New Zealand?"

My dad replied without hesitation, "I would be willing to do whatever job available to me to support my family."

She replied, "Great! We will inform you again about the next phase, the health screening."

My dad asked for affirmation, "Does this mean we pass this interview today?"

She replied, "Yes and congratulations."

We said thank you to Diane and left the meeting filled with joy.

On our way back to the house, Dad said, "Let's go and get a chicken. We should celebrate tonight."

And we did. It was the first time we had a whole chicken for dinner since we had come to Camp Khao I Dang eighteen months ago.

I know some of you may not comprehend what a big deal it was to have a whole chicken for dinner. You see, during our stay in the camp, my parents and all other refugees had no employment and thus no income. Although we may still have some money, we did not know how long we needed to stay in the camp for and if we would get a chance to migrate to a new country at all. So we needed to make our money last as long as we could.

Three weeks later, about early July 1981, we saw our name on the notice board again, this time for health screening. Fortunately we also made it through with no problems, and we were notified that we would be leaving the camp on August 21, 1981, going to New Zealand.

It was now August 21, 1981. We were scheduled to meet at the camp front office at 10:00 a.m. to wait for the bus to take us to Bangkok. We could not sleep at all last night, as we were so excited and still could not believe this was the last night we would stay at the refugee camp.

We got to the front office by 9:30 a.m. Twelve other families were also gathered at the front office, waiting for the bus. The bus showed up at about 9:45 a.m., and we departed on time, heading to Bangkok.

As we left Camp Khao I Dang, we did not have our itinerary. We just assumed we were heading to Bangkok to take a flight to New Zealand. We arrived in Bangkok around 1:00 p.m. I was very excited to see a bustling Bangkok city, and the street was full of energy as the bus snaked through Bangkok traffic. Soon the bus slowed down, and I saw the bus enter a compound or some kind of institution. The compound was surrounded by a tall cement fence with barbed wire on top of the fence.

We were told to get off the bus here, and we were escorted to our temporary room to stay for the next few days. Inside there were two rows of rooms in a long-shaped building. Each room or cell had cement walls on three sides with no window, and there was no furniture, just bare floor (no table, chair, bench, and bed), and each room could house four to eight people.

Now, I could tell this compound was in fact a former jail, as I could see holes on the floor and wall where the metal bars used to be. Each family was assigned to stay in a cell. We could move around and chat freely with other refugees inside the building. We now had electricity, running water, and a common facilities down the hall. A Thai food catering contractor would bring in meals for us, three times per day.

Eight

Freedom at Last in New Zealand

Three days went past in no time. Once again we could not sleep the last night because we were so excited and still could not believe we got this once-in-a-lifetime opportunity to resettle in a new country, New Zealand.

We all woke up before dawn and got ready. We got on the bus and the bus departed on time before sunrise, heading to Bangkok International Airport. A New Zealand immigration staff member came to meet us at the airport. He handed each family the plane tickets and our itinerary to New Zealand as we got off the bus.

Now we could see. First we would take a Thai Airway from Bangkok to Singapore. We would arrive in Singapore about noon. We would have four hours in transit in the Singapore airport. Then we would take Air New Zealand from Singapore to Auckland, New Zealand. And we would arrive in Auckland about 8:00 a.m. the next day.

We checked in and got our boarding pass, and the New Zealand immigration staff member brought us to a special lane, bypassing the regular passport check. He told us later we went through a special lane because we did not have passports. He took us to the gate and checked off each family member name on the list as we entered the plane.

I was so excited to enter the plane, as it was my first time. My brother and I were seated in a center row; my parents were seated on the same row but to our left, near the window. I was very curious and wanted to press every button I saw. But my dad told us not to touch anything. Soon the plane took off, and the flight attendant began meal service about twenty minutes later.

The flight attendant asked, "Would you like Thai fried rice or egg and sausage?"

I assumed the meal would be quite expensive, and since we had no money, I told her, "No, because I got no money."

The nice flight attendant explained, "All meals, coffee, tea, and water are free."

I replied, "Free. I like Thai fried rice, please."

My brother also chose Thai fried rice. I excitedly told my parents that meals and drinks were free. The flight attendant brought me Thai fried rice, served on fancy Thai Airway plates with shining forks and spoons.

Next the flight attendant asked my parents what they would like to have.

My dad replied in broken English, "Free. OK, fried rice and coffee."

My mom also had Thai fried rice. The flight to Singapore was not too long. In fact, while the flight attendants were still collecting the meal trays, the captain announced we were preparing for landing. We soon landed and docked at the terminal in the Singapore airport. We, the refugees heading to New Zealand, were asked to remain seated while other passengers got off the plane.

A New Zealand immigration staff member came in and greeted us inside the plane. She then walked us to the waiting room at the gate for our next flight. She asked us to wait there. She also showed us the facilities in the terminal. She added we had about three hours, so we could walk around this terminal but not to wander far. And she reminded us that we must be back at this gate one hour before departure time.

I told Dad I would walk around to explore nearby. The airport was very modern and the cleanest place I had ever seen in my whole life. The waiting room chairs and tables were spotlessly clean, and the marble floor was shining. My dad and I went to look at some of the electronic appliance stores inside the terminal. There were all kinds of exciting electronics I had never seen before (cameras, CD players, boom boxes, and digital watches). Most of them were Japanese brands.

We went back to our gate and waited for our next flight. I saw a huge Air New Zealand plane come in and dock at our gate. It was a beautiful plane, and I could not wait to see the inside. Soon it was time to board the plane, and the plane departed right on time, heading to Auckland.

We flew across the Pacific overnight and arrived at Auckland International Airport the next morning. I got a window seat on this journey. I was able to look out as the plane was descending. From above, all I saw were two big islands in front and a big ocean. Soon the plane landed. The flight attendant requested us, the group of refugees, to wait inside the plane while other passengers disembarked. Soon a couple of New Zealand immigration staff members came to greet us at the gate as we exited the plane.

Again we were taken through a special lane and made our way to a waiting bus outside the airport. Once we were on board the bus, they welcomed us to New Zealand and told us it was now about 9:00 a.m. local time, and people changed the time on their watches. They also told us we are going to a resettlement center not too far, just outside the airport.

The bus arrived at Mangare Refugee Resettlement center about twenty minutes later. Mangare is the name of this town just outside the airport. The compound looked like a hostel that had recently turned into a refugee resettlement center. It had two one-floor buildings for accommodation. Each building had about thirty rooms, and each room can take two people. The site also had two big halls, one for a dining room and another for a recreation room. There were also four to five classrooms and one administration office.

My parents got a room; my brother and I also got a room next door. After we dropped our bags inside our room, we all went to the recreation hall for a briefing. There a director of New Zealand immigration and her staff welcomed us. She gave us a brief introduction about our stay in this transition hostel. She said over the next six weeks, we would attend classes each day to learn about life in New Zealand, like how and where to pay the bills. I thought they should probably skip this session, so I could use it as an excuse for delay in paying my bill. (Just kidding.) We also learned how to get a driving license and how to look for information in the phone book.

There was no internet or Google search in 1981. Everything you needed to find—utility companies, social service departments, restaurants, Department of Motor Vehicles, etc.—were categorized in the phone book. They were organized alphabetically in a phone book with hundreds of pages. We were also introduced to New Zealand government structure, our rights as New Zealand residents, schooling systems, and other social services available. We would also be offered English lessons during our stay in this hostel.

Soon it was lunchtime, and we were led to the dining hall to get lunch. Each person would pick up a clean tray, utensils, and napkin. We then walked to the food counter to get our food. Kitchen staff stood behind the counter, ready to serve us food, our first New Zealand meal. I walked up with my tray. A kitchen staff handed me a plate with a whole fried flounder, fish.

I was very shocked and happy that I was given such a big fish for myself. You see, in a Cambodian meal, this fish would need to be shared with the whole family. In fact, I never had a whole fish for a meal by myself in my whole life. He then asked if I liked mashed potatoes or fries. I did not know what fries were. But I saw mashed potatoes in one tray and a string of fried potatoes in the next tray. I pointed to the fried potatoes.

He asked to confirm, "You want some fries, right?"

By now, I had figured out the string of fried potatoes was called fries. I said, "Yes, please."

After the meal, we had the whole afternoon free to rest and explore the compound. Each person was given a winter jacket and a pair of warm pants since August was winter in New Zealand.

When I woke up the next morning, I did not feel cold at all since the room was heated. I forgot about the warm jacket given to each of us. But when I opened the door and tried to go to the dining hall, I was shaken by how cold it was. I quickly went back to the room to put on another layer and ran to the dining hall. Breakfast was served at 7:00 a.m. We had so many choices for breakfast: coffee, English tea, boiled eggs, fried or scrambled eggs, bacon, toast, cereal, oatmeal, and fresh fruit.

For refugee orientation, we were split into four groups: one class for men, one class for women, one class for teenagers aged fourteen to twenty years old, and another class for children. And the class started at 9:00 a.m. and finished at 3:00 p.m. By week five, the hostel took us out for an Auckland city tour. We went to see Auckland downtown and the Auckland Museum and visited local beaches.

Soon we completed our six-week stay at the hostel, and our sponsor came to take us to our new home. Each family was sponsored by a volunteer New Zealand family or church group, coming from different parts of New Zealand, some in Auckland, a few in Wellington, the capital city, and others in Christchurch or Dunedin in the South Island.

On the evening before the final day at the hostel, we had a party with cultural dance and talent shows, a way to express our appreciation to the director of New Zealand immigration and her staff, who made us so welcome and assisted us in our transition.

The next morning, each New Zealand sponsor came to pick up their newcomers. We said thank you and goodbye to the hostel management and all the staff. We also said goodbye and best wishes to our refugee friends.

Our sponsor, Mr. Ly, was from Auckland. He drove us to our new home in a suburb called Otara. We got to Otara about thirty minutes later. We were taken to an apartment complex, a government-subsidized rental unit. This was a block with many buildings. Our building had four units, two on the ground floor and two on the second floor.

We got a unit on the second floor. Our unit had three bedrooms, one bathroom, a living room, and a kitchen. Mr. Ly showed us to the unit. It had been furnished with beds, a sofa, and some basic household items (blankets, towels, plates, cooking pots, etc.). Honestly, this house was better than any place I had ever lived in the past ten years. He had even filled our fridge with meat, vegetables, and fruits.

We were deeply touched by his kindness and attentive arrangement. He told us today was Friday and that we had a couple of days to get settled. Next Monday, he would come back and bring my brother and me to enroll at the local high school. He would also bring my parents to get some interviews for jobs. And he gave us his home phone, just in case we needed to call him. And I almost forgot, the house also had an active phone line. To us, this was a big deal at the time.

We spent the next couple of days settling down. We walked around and checked out the neighborhood. We found the Otara market center about two blocks away. There, they also had a flea market every Saturday morning, where local farmers sold fresh produce and fisherman sold their fresh catch.

The weekend went by quickly. Mr. Ly came back on Monday morning. He took my brother and me to enroll in a local school called Otara High School. My brother and I started school the next day. The school was about a mile away, so we walked to school every day. For the first few weeks, we had many challenges at school. We could not follow most subjects due to poor English and no formal schooling.

After our school enrollment, Mr. Ly took Mom and Dad to a local employment agency to look for jobs. He also helped both to land a job within two weeks. Mom worked at a local bakery factory. They made meat pies, doughnuts, and other cakes for the supermarket. Dad got a job as a janitor at a Ford Motor Assembly plant.

Although both positions were not fancy, Mom and Dad were happy with their jobs, and it helped us to be independent. Dad said, "We do what we need to do." And they were happy that we, my brother and I, finally got a chance to go to school.

Fast-forward twenty-eight years later. My wife and I like to watch a television show called *The Big Bang Theory*. We were watching one of the episodes sometime in 2019 in which Howard threw Sheldon a quantum mechanic question, and Sheldon did not know the answer. A Caltech, California Institute of Technology, janitor happened to be in the same room. The janitor gave out the correct answer while he was cleaning the floor.

But Sheldon shut him off. "You are a janitor. What do you know about quantum mechanics?"

The janitor replied, "Here I am a janitor, but back in Ukraine, I was a nuclear physicist."

I wiped away a tear after the scene.

My wife saw it and asked, "Did you cry?"

I told her, "Don't worry. It was a tear of joy."

But in reality, that scene touched me, as it reminded me about my parents, especially my dad. They gave up everything—home, jobs, and savings—to become refugees and finally move to New Zealand so my brother and I could get an education and a better life. Thank you, Mom and Dad.

Back to New Zealand in 1981. About four weeks after we settled in Otara, one day when I opened the front door to go out, I saw a white lady who happened to drop by to see our neighbor, Mr. Tran, a former Vietnamese refugee who came to New Zealand a few months before us. She introduced herself as Margaret McComb.

We found out Margaret was Mr. Tran's sponsor. We chatted for a few minutes with my broken English and poor grammar. But Margaret was very patient with me. She lifted my confidence to converse with her. I told her we were Cambodian refugees and had just come to New Zealand a few weeks ago. She asked which school my brother and I planned to attend. I told her Mr. Ly, our sponsor, had enrolled us at Otara High School, two blocks from here.

Margaret asked, "If you are OK with it, I can help you enroll in a better school called Otahuhu College."

I told her we needed to check with Mr. Ly first. Margaret asked for Mr. Ly's phone number. Margaret later called Mr. Ly and asked if she could enroll us at Otahuhu College.

Mr. Ly replied, "Otahuhu College would be a better school. But it's in a different school district." He was not sure we could get into Otahuhu College.

Margaret said, "No worry. I used to be a teacher there. Let me talk to the school principal."

The following Monday, Margaret called and said she had talked to the school principal at Otahuhu College. They had agreed to accept us. The next morning, Margaret came to take both my brother and me to Otahuhu College to complete the enrollment. We told the school we both preferred to be in the same class since we could help each other out. The school compassionately accepted our request.

We enrolled in Form 4 at Otahuhu College, based on my age. Form 4 is equivalent to second year in high school or ninth grade. Margaret was so kind that she even bought my brother and me our first pair of Otahuhu College school uniforms.

It was now October, and the New Zealand school year would end in five weeks. At this time of the year, many classes had school camping trips for students, and this had been arranged many weeks ago. Since we had just arrived, there was no time to make any arrangements for us to join the camping trip.

So for the next few weeks, my brother and I were sent to different classes. We did not mind, as we were too new to the school, plus we could not follow the classes anyway due to poor English and no formal schooling. Soon the school year ended, and there was no more school for the next three months.

Margaret helped me to land a summer job at a local supermarket chain called Foodtown Supermarket. I started working there as grocery packer behind the cashier. I liked the job because I was able to meet and talk to many customers. There were plenty of chances to practice my English. I continued to work at Foodtown as a part-time student worker after that summer. In fact, I ended up working part-time at Foodtown Supermarket for the next ten years while I was studying in high school and college.

Summer holiday quickly went by, and a new school year began. My brother and I started a new year in Form 5. We took five subjects: English, math, physics, chemistry, and economics. We had many challenges in the first semester due to poor English and new subjects. They were new subjects because we had never attended any formal school until now.

To give you some idea how bad we were, for English, we had limited vocabulary and poor grammar. For Math, we knew basic arithmetic, but we did not know how to multiply negative numbers or do trigonometry, and my brother and I were about 14 and 15 years old respectively at the time. For physics and chemistry, we were totally lost. We had never seen a periodic table and had no idea what the elements were. But all the teachers were very patient and kind to us. Many of our teachers offered to go over our homework during their lunchtime. So my brother and I spent our lunchtime in a classroom with one teacher per day: Monday, English; Tuesday, math; and so on.

Three months into the new school year, we learned that Form 5 was a very crucial year for high school students because at the end of the year, we needed to take a national examination called the School Certificate. It was an exam for all Form 5 students set by the New Zealand Education Department. And this School Certificate is a force-ranking system. This means only 50 percent of the students were allowed to move on. In New Zealand, if a student failed to make the grade for the School Certificate, he or she would likely finish school and get out to find a job.

My parents did not pressure my brother or me on schoolwork. Maybe they clearly understood the challenges we had, not just with English but with every subject. I was fully aware of my weaknesses. But I was also willing to try my best.

We were now six months into Form 5, and it was time to take the midyear exam. Our grades were borderline. Our teachers told us we did well, given the circumstances. Maybe they were too polite or did not want to discourage us. Anyway, I knew I still had six months to work and improve my grades for the final School Certificate examinations. So we continued to work hard and spend our lunchtime with teachers.

Finally it was time for my brother and me to face the music. The final year School Certificate exam had arrived. We went to a big school hall to take our examination. The exam was supervised by staff from the New Zealand Education Department, not our own teachers. Since New Zealand is a multicultural society, to prevent any racial bias, all students taking this national School Certificate exam were given a personal identification number. Each exam paper would be logged with a unique personal ID, not a name. We had five subjects, and our examination was spread into two-week periods.

After completing the School Certificate examination, we had to wait several weeks for the results. I went to find a summer job at a local factory while we waited for the results to come by mail. Four weeks later, my brother and I each received our School Certificate result. We opened each envelope nervously. We were so happy to see we had made it past the School Certificate in all subjects. In fact, we did well in math, physics, and chemistry, and OK in economics and English.

We could tell our parents were also happy, as many of our peers, either Otahuhu classmates or former Cambodian refugee kids, could not pass this step. After all, nationally, only about 50 percent of the students could pass it by design.

We moved on to continue our schooling in Form 6. We continued to make good progress with our English and other subjects. Somehow we went on to win a scholarship at Form 6. The Otahuhu Rotary Club sponsored the scholarship. They selected the top four students from Otahuhu College and four students from another local high school called King College. Incredibly, my brother and I made the list from Otahuhu College. This was a very big surprise and a confidence booster for my brother and me and I guess anyone who knew us. Remember, this was our second year in school after we had arrived in New Zealand with virtually no formal education and not much English.

The prize was a two-week sailing trip on a yacht out to different islands on the Hauraki Gulf. We were very happy and honored to be the winners. But our excitement and joy quickly turned to become our dilemma. We learned that we needed to bring sleeping bags to join the group. Frankly, we did not even know what a sleeping bag was, nor what it was for. We later learned we needed a sleeping bag to keep us warm when we slept on a yacht, and it would cost $150 each. This was very expensive to us at the time. I knew Dad and Mom were making only $5 or $6 per hour. And $300 would be enough to buy groceries for a whole week.

My brother and I discussed and decided to let the school know we could not go sailing. We did not tell our parents because we knew they were working hard to support the family and they were saving every penny in hopes to get our own first home in our new country. To us, clearly sailing should be a low priority compared to getting your own house.

The sailing trip was still two weeks away. My brother and I told our teacher, Ms. Cleary, that we were sorry but we could not go on the sailing trip. Ms. Cleary was shocked to hear we did not want to go on a sailing trip, as many kids would kill to get selected. We explained our dilemma.

We told Ms. Cleary on a Monday. By Wednesday, we were told the school principal, Mr. Owen Boscawen, would like to see us in his office at lunchtime. My brother and I were nervous and did not know what to expect. We went to the principal's office, and his secretary brought us to see him. We had seen Mr. Boscawen in the school many times during the school assembly meeting or walking in the hallway, but we had not spoken to him in person. We did not know what to expect.

When Mr. Boscawen saw us coming in as his secretary opened the door, he greeted us and immediately offered us sandwiches for lunch. We sat down nervously but still did not know why he wanted to see us. He asked about our schoolwork.

"When did you come to New Zealand? Do you like New Zealand?" And so on as if he knew we were nervous. He tried to put us at ease. Eventually he said, "I learned you both cannot join the upcoming Rotary Club sailing trip."

By now we figured Ms. Cleary must have talked to him about our sailing trip dilemma. I explained to him that we were very grateful and honored to be selected for the scholarship. But we just could not go.

He nodded. "I know," he said as if he understood and were going to accept our declination.

But two days later, we were again told Mr. Boscawen would like to see us in his office on Friday at lunchtime. We showed up at his office again. He offered us sandwiches, and then he walked to one of his office cabinets. He opened the cabinet and pulled out two bags.

He said, "Boys, here are your sleeping bags. I hope you now can join the other boys on the sailing trip and have some fun." He passed one bag to me and the other bag to my brother.

We were speechless and so touched by his generosity. We said, "Thank you so much, Mr. Boscawen."

The next morning, we joined the other boys and went sailing on a yacht for two weeks on the Hauraki Gulf. This was our first time ever to go sailing on a yacht. We stopped by a few remote islands, we went scuba diving, we caught some lobsters, we had a picnic on one of the islands, and we also made new friends and fond memories.

Soon a new school year began. We proceeded to study for the university entrance exam and got accepted to the Engineering School at the University of Auckland. My brother and I went on to complete our college courses and obtain our degrees. My brother landed a job in Auckland City and settled in New Zealand, while I went to work in Singapore for three years and later moved to the United States. And as they say, the rest is history.

Thank you for your interest in my stories, and I hope you enjoyed the reading.

The photo was taken, in 1970, prior to
Albert's mom mysterious departure and
Albert was the taller boy on the left.

The photo was taken post Pol Pot regime in 1979,
after the boys re-united with mom 9 years later.

Family photos, the top photo was taken in
Refugee camp, Khao I Dang in 1979

This family photo was taken in Auckland
New Zealand in 1986.

This photo was taken with Barbara Moore at Otahuhu
College after the Form6 Scholarship ceremony.

Printed in the United States
By Bookmasters